Microwave Magic
Entertaining

Grolier Limited
TORONTO

Contributors to this series:

Recipes and Technical Assistance:
École de cuisine Bachand-Bissonnette
Cooking consultants:
Denis Bissonette
Michèle Émond
Dietician:
Christiane Barbeau
Photos:
Laramée Morel Communications
Audio-Visuelles
Design:
Claudette Taillefer
Assistants:
Julie Deslauriers
Philippe O'Connor
Joan Pothier
Accessories:
Andrée Cournoyer
Writing:
Communications La Griffe Inc.
Text Consultants:
Cap et bc inc.
Advisors:
Roger Aubin
Joseph R. De Varennes
Gaston Lavoie
Kenneth H. Pearson

Assembly:
Carole Garon
Vital Lapalme
Jean-Pierre Larose
Carl Simmons
Gus Soriano
Marc Vallières
Production Managers:
Gilles Chamberland
Ernest Homewood
Production Assistants:
Martine Gingras
Catherine Gordon
Kathy Kishimoto
Peter Thomlison
Art Director:
Bernard Lamy
Editors:
Laurielle Ilacqua
Susan Marshall
Margaret Oliver
Robin Rivers
Lois Rock
Jocelyn Smyth
Donna Thomson
Dolores Williams
Development:
Le Groupe Polygone Éditeurs Inc.

We wish to thank the following firms, PIER I IMPORTS and LE CACHE POT, for their contribution to the illustration of this set.

The series editors have taken every care to ensure that the information given is accurate. However, no cookbook can guarantee the user successful results. The editors cannot accept any responsibility for the results obtained by following the recipes and recommendations given.

Canadian Cataloguing in Publication Data

Main entry under title:

Entertaining

(Microwave magic ; 25)
Translation of: Fêtes et réceptions.
Includes index.
ISBN 0-7172-2446-5

1. Entertaining.   2. Microwave cookery.
I. Series: Microwave magic (Toronto, Ont.) ; 25.

TX832.F4813 1988   641.5'68   C88-094224-X

Contents

Microwave Magic is a multi-volume set, with each volume devoted to a particular type of cooking. So, if you are looking for a chicken recipe, you simply go to one of the two volumes that deal with poultry. Each volume has its own index, and the final volume contains a general index to the complete set.

Microwave Magic puts over twelve hundred recipes at your fingertips. You will find it as useful as the microwave oven itself. Enjoy!

Note from the Editor

How to Use this Book

The books in this set have been designed to make your job as easy as possible. As a result, most of the recipes are set out in a standard way.

We suggest that you begin by consulting the information chart for the recipe you have chosen. You will find there all the information you need to decide if you are able to make it: preparation time, cost per serving, level of difficulty, number of calories per serving and other relevant details. Thus, if you have only 30 minutes in which to prepare the evening meal, you will quickly be able to tell which recipe is possible and suits your schedule.

The list of ingredients is always clearly separated from the main text. When space allows, the ingredients are shown together in a photograph so that you can make sure you have them all without rereading the list—

another way of saving your valuable time. In addition, for the more complex recipes we have supplied photographs of the key stages involved either in preparation or serving.

All the dishes in this book have been cooked in a 700 watt microwave oven. If your oven has a different wattage, consult the conversion chart that appears on the following page for cooking times in different types of oven. We would like to emphasize that the cooking times given in the book are a minimum. If a dish does not seem to be cooked enough, you may return it to the oven for a few more minutes. Also, the cooking time can vary according to your ingredients: their water and fat content, thickness, shape and even where they come from. We have therefore left a blank space on each recipe page in which you can note

the cooking time that suits you best. This will enable you to add a personal touch to the recipes that we suggest and to reproduce your best results every time.

Although we have put all the technical information together at the front of this book, we have inserted a number of boxed entries called **MICROTIPS** throughout to explain particular techniques. They are brief and simple, and will help you obtain successful results in your cooking.

With the very first recipe you try, you will discover just how simple microwave cooking can be and how often it depends on techniques you already use for cooking with a conventional oven. If cooking is a pleasure for you, as it is for us, it will be all the more so with a microwave oven. Now let's get on with the food.

The Editor

Key to the Symbols

For ease of reference, the following symbols have been used on the recipe information charts.

The pencil symbol ✏️ is a reminder to write your cooking time in the space provided.

Level of Difficulty

🍴 Easy

🍴🍴 Moderate

🍴🍴🍴 Complex

Cost per Serving

$ Inexpensive

$ $ Moderate

$ $ $ Expensive

Power Levels

All the recipes in this book have been tested in a 700 watt oven. As there are many microwave ovens on the market with different power levels, and as the names of these levels vary from one manufacturer to another, we have decided to give power levels as a percentage. To adapt the power levels given here, consult the chart opposite and the instruction manual for your oven.

Generally speaking, if you have a 500 watt or 600 watt oven you should increase cooking times by about 30% over those given, depending on the actual length of time required. The shorter the original cooking time, the greater the percentage by which it must be lengthened. The 30% figure is only an average. Consult the chart for detailed information on this topic.

Power Levels

HIGH: 100% - 90%	Vegetables (except boiled potatoes and carrots) Soup Sauce Fruits Browning ground beef Browning dish Popcorn
MEDIUM HIGH: 80% - 70%	Rapid defrosting of precooked dishes Muffins Some cakes Hot dogs
MEDIUM: 60% - 50%	Cooking tender meat Cakes Fish Seafood Eggs Reheating Boiled potatoes and carrots
MEDIUM LOW: 40%	Cooking less tender meat Simmering Melting chocolate
DEFROST: 30% **LOW: 30% - 20%**	Defrosting Simmering Cooking less tender meat
WARM: 10%	Keeping food warm Allowing yeast dough to rise

Cooking Time Conversion Chart

700 watts	600 watts*
5 s	11 s
15 s	20 s
30 s	40 s
45 s	1 min
1 min	1 min 20 s
2 min	2 min 40 s
3 min	4 min
4 min	5 min 20 s
5 min	6 min 40 s
6 min	8 min
7 min	9 min 20 s
8 min	10 min 40 s
9 min	12 min
10 min	13 min 30 s
20 min	26 min 40 s
30 min	40 min
40 min	53 min 40 s
50 min	66 min 40 s
1 h	1 h 20 min

* There is very little difference in cooking times between 500 watt ovens and 600 watt ovens.

Entertaining

The Pleasure of Entertaining Guests

Important events and family parties have always been celebrated around the table. We can all remember an especially successful event: a birthday, wedding reception, Christmas party, important business meal or fun-filled get-together. All around the world, and throughout history, meals have been at the center of the best conversations, the most important meetings or simply, the happiest friendships.

When people entertain, they like to offer their guests the very best they have, in both food and drink. Add to that a welcoming atmosphere, a beautifully decorated table and pleasant conversation and the event is sure to be not only a great success but also a joy for the guests and hosts alike.

A successful party is certain to warm hearts and seal friendships.

Banquets

Thin is in and people are conscientious about what they eat. Microwave cooking lets you feast regularly without worrying about the consequences because it uses very little fat and preserves all a food's nutritional qualities. Microwave cooking also comes to the rescue of those who are too busy to devote a lot of time to cooking.

Today, most kitchens are equipped with two unbeatable appliances; the microwave oven and the freezer. Thanks to them, you can quickly prepare a feast several days before the big event: just freeze the foods and when needed, defrost and reheat them. You can be sure that the flavor and quality will not be altered. Since most of the meat will have been prepared in advance on the big day, the hosts will only have to do last minute preparations, while the guests enjoy the appetizers. No more stress caused by trying to prepare a party while balancing work, children and household chores. With a microwave oven, the relaxed cook can join the party with a smile!

The microwave oven and the freezer are also very useful when unexpected guests arrive. From now on you can enjoy this surprise party, without worrying about whether you have enough time to prepare a meal; everything can be defrosted and prepared in no time.

Of course, a microwave oven lets you spend less time in the kitchen. And it also provides another undeniable advantages: it lets you cook when you have the time . . . and the inclination. If, on a Saturday afternoon, you have the urge to prepare an Emincé of Veal with Cream Sauce and a Mocha Cake, but you have not yet sent out any invitations, go ahead! Prepare the meal and invite your friends for the following Saturday: the freezer/microwave duo is there to help you!

Decorating the Table

A simple meal can be transformed into a memorable event if you take the time to present it with care. A few little touches are enough. Often, the foods themselves can be used as decoration. At other times, the serving dishes or other elements on the table can be decorated.

Food Decoration

You don't need a gold-rimmed set of china or Japanese-style floral arrangements to add a special touch to your table: a bit of imagination, a surprising touch and the decoration is complete. Knowing how to make use of foods, their textures, shapes and colors and knowing how to combine them, you can create a beautiful table; decorate your dishes with bouquets of parsley, slices of lemon, radishes, and strips of red or green pepper. Make one course the centerpiece; consider using different shapes of bread or fruits, a splendid cake or a bowl of nuts. Fruits and vegetables, such as gourds, tomatoes and eggplants can add bright colors to your table: rub them first with vegetable oil to make them shine.

Table Accessories

Bouquets of flowers are often used to decorate a table and always add a happy note to any meal, but it is important to take care when arranging the flowers. Choose a bouquet that is not too tall; after all, your guests will want to see each other. To add a special touch to your small bouquets, use unusual vases, such as an old teapot, for example. If you have enough space, put a flower at each guest's place.

No fruits or vegetables available? Too late to run to the florist? House plants can make a useful contribution. Just wrap the pot in pretty paper and use it as a centerpiece.

Table runners, those long, narrow cloths which cover a table from one end to the other, can also be used as decoration. Placed at the center of the table, they protect the area where the serving dishes are put down. For special occasions, make a little extra effort: use your nicest dishes and cutlery and your best tablecloths. If you use a colored tablecloth, put a pretty lace napkin at the center of the table. Take care to harmonize the shapes and colors of the napkins and tablecloth.

Use tablecloths, napkins and flowers all in the same color to create an interesting effect. Here's another trick: if you are preparing a theme party, an Italian evening for example, decorate the table with the colors of the Italian flag: red, white and green. Play with the shape of the dinner napkins; arrange them in wine glasses. Don't be afraid to use your imagination; buy gold- or silver-colored paper napkins or sprinkle the tablecloth with confetti.

You can also arrange different sizes and shapes of candles at the center of the table or at each guest's place to create an enchanting lighting effect. You might need to protect the table or the cloth from flame and dripping wax by putting a saucer under the candle. And make sure that the flame is at eye level or lower so as not to disturb your guests' view.

Decoration is especially important for children's parties. Clowns, magic and excitement are the ingredients for these events where the presentation of the meal and the table decorations all add to a child's joy. We can all remember favorite children's parties with a whole bunch of excited and happy little friends. And because of all the excitement, it's best to set the table with only the essentials. Don't use any fragile or breakable objects. If possible, serve the meal in a room without carpeting and choose a location that's easy to clean. Once you have taken these few precautions, you can use all the little gadgets made for children's parties: balloons, whistles, etc.

Setting the Table

If you have invited many people, arrange your buffet on a large table in two rows, with the same dishes on each side of the table; this way the guests can serve themselves face to face.

Buffet or Sit Down Dinner?

Which is more suitable? It all depends on your guests, on how many people you have invited and how much preparation you want to do. If you have invited a large number of people, a buffet is more appropriate. Usually buffets are laid out on a long table and the guests help themselves to the food, which they take away from the table to eat. The main problems to foresee are space and circulation. If the room is large enough, put the table in the middle of the room or far enough away from the wall that guests can circulate around it. Set the buffet so that guests move around the table in a clockwise direction. Lay out the dishes in the right order, starting of course with the plates. If you are serving a hot meal, place the main dish first, then follow with vegetables, salad, condiments, rolls and finally, the serviettes and cutlery.

If the room is smaller, push the table against the wall and set the buffet along the length of the table. The desserts and coffee can be arranged on another table or passed around, if you prefer not to set the table for this

Notes
1. Make sure you have sufficient paper plates, serviettes and cutlery.
2. Leave sufficient space between the serving dishes so that guests can put down their plates and serve themselves more comfortably.
3. Don't forget to have a place where guests can leave their dishes when they have finished eating.
4. Keep some cleaning solvent and a brush handy to clean up any little spills. You can never protect yourself completely from little messes.

MICROTIPS

For Successful Entertaining

Every dinner party needs very careful planning and a lot of preparation which should not be done in haste, at the last minute. And all the special efforts taken should not be forgotten after a couple of days. For all these reasons, it's a good idea to keep some notes on each party you give. For example, keep your shopping list and later add to it the provisions you were missing.

It's also a good idea to make a note of the order and time you prepared each step of the meal to avoid any timing problems in the future. This is the way to succeed at every party and to keep improving.

last part of the meal.

And what about traditional meals and their presentation? Whether elaborate or relaxed, protocol is much simpler than it was in the past. The place setting is now much more limited. There is really no need any more to use a plate for bread. And if salad is served at the same time as the main dish, only one fork is required. You may also put the soup bowl on a saucer on top of the dinner plate.

The rules governing cutlery often cause consternation among guests invited for the first time to a dinner party; many guests choose to wait until their neighbors begin eating to know which fork to use. But the rule is really quite simple; cutlery is set out in the order in which the courses are served, and is used in that order. The cutlery placed the furthest out is the first to be used and so on to the last piece. For example, if you start the meal with a soup, put the soup spoon at the far right.

1. Salad plate
2. Water glass
3. Wine glass
4. Fork
5. Dessert fork
6. Dinner plate
7. Serviette
8. Small knife (for bread)
9. Large knife
10. Teaspoon
11. Soup spoon
12. Bread plate (optional)
13. Space for the soup bowl, when served (on the dinner plate)

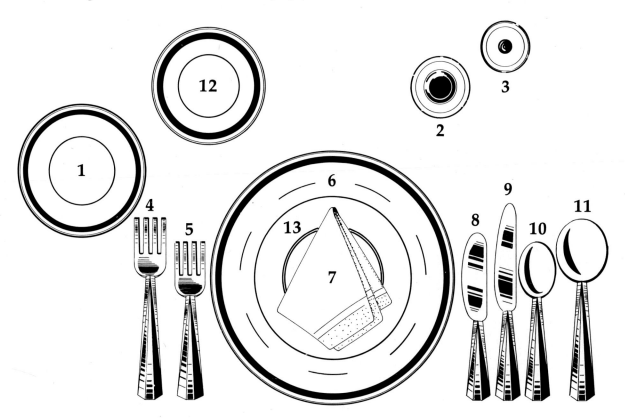

Punches

Punches—what a delicious way to quench a thirst while discovering the most unexpected flavors! Served in a large bowl set in the middle of the table, your punch will immediately become the center of attention for the evening, drawing your guests together and helping them get to know each other.

Punches can be made with rum, champagne or wine, flavored with kirsch, cognac or armagnac, spiced with lemon or cinnamon and garnished with pineapple, strawberries or oranges; there's a punch to please every taste! Try Sangria, a red wine and fruit concoction from Spain, or our Japanese punch, made with sake and ginger. Tasted and sampled, each one will enliven the conversation.

Fortunately, punches made without alcohol are also delicious. And more and more hosts, concerned about their guests well-being and safety, are offering a non-alcoholic punch for those who prefer to avoid alcohol. These colorful and delicious drinks add a festive touch to any get-together and are enjoyed by all. Cheers!

Golden Punch*

Ingredients
2 bottles champagne
2 bottles sweet white wine, Sauterne type
1 bottle soda water
2 bags ice cubes
60 mL (2 oz) cognac
60 mL (2 oz) cointreau
50 mL (1/4 cup) maple syrup
250 mL (1 cup) strawberries, finely chopped
fresh mint leaves, to taste

Method
— In a large bowl, combine the champagne, white wine and soda water; refrigerate for 12 hours.
— Put the ice cubes in a punch bowl; combine the cognac, cointreau and maple syrup and pour over the ice cubes; stir.
— Add the mixture of champagne, wine and soda water.
— Garnish with strawberries and mint leaves before serving.

* **Refrigerate for 12 hours before serving.**

Flamboyant Punch*

Ingredients
5 L (160 oz) rosé wine
1 bottle sparkling white wine
185 mL (6 oz) cognac
185 mL (6 oz) kirsch
450 g (1 lb) frozen raspberries
450 g (1 lb) frozen strawberries

Method
— In a punch bowl, combine all the ingredients and mix well.
— Refrigerate.

* **Refrigerate for several hours before serving.**

Fruit Punch*

Ingredients
1 small pineapple, cubed
15 red grapes, cut in half
15 green grapes, cut in half
15 strawberries, cut in half
15 raspberries, whole
500 mL (2 cups) brandy
500 mL (2 cups) cointreau
3 to 4 bottles very dry white wine

Method
— In a large bowl, combine all the fruits, brandy and cointreau; marinate overnight.
— Remove 250 mL (1 cup) of the mixture and pour into a crown mold.
— Add white wine to fill up the mold and freeze for 24 hours.
— Put the frozen mold into a large punch bowl, add the marinated fruits and the remaining wine.

* **Marinate the fruits overnight and freeze for 24 hours.**

Champagne Punch*

Ingredients
2 bottles champagne
1/2 pineapple, cut in pieces
8 red grapes, cut in half
8 green grapes, cut in half
8 strawberries, cut in half
8 raspberries, cut in half
250 mL (1 cup) apricot brandy
250 mL (1 cup) cointreau

Method
— In a large bowl, combine all the fruits, brandy and cointreau; marinate for 12 hours.
— Remove 250 mL (1 cup) of the mixture and pour into a crown mold.
— Add champagne to fill up the mold and freeze for 24 hours.
— Put the frozen crown into a large punch bowl, add the marinated fruits and the remaining champagne.

* **Marinate the fruits for 12 hours and freeze for 24 hours.**

Mulled Wine

Ingredients
3 bottles red wine
1 L (4 cups) water
3 sticks cinnamon
8 cloves
300 mL (1-1/4 cups) orange syrup
150 mL (2/3 cup) lemon syrup
3 oranges, sliced

Method
— In a large dish combine the water, cinnamon and cloves; heat at 100% for 10 to 12 minutes.
— Strain and add the orange syrup, lemon syrup and wine.
— Heat at 100% for 8 to 10 minutes.
— Garnish with slices of orange before serving.

Japanese Punch*

Ingredients
625 mL (2-1/2 cups) steeped tea
4 cloves
2 sticks cinnamon
5 mL (1 teaspoon) ground ginger
sake to taste
2.5 L (10 cups) fresh lemonade
ice cubes
mint sprigs, for garnish

Method
— In a bowl, combine the tea, cloves, cinnamon and ginger; heat at 100% for 5 minutes.
— Let cool completely and strain into a punch bowl.
— Add the sake and lemonade; add the ice cubes to cool the mixture and garnish with mint sprigs before serving.

* Cool the mixture before serving.

Sangria*

Ingredients
1 bottle Spanish red wine
30 mL (2 tablespoons) sugar
1/2 lemon, sliced
1 orange, sliced
60 mL (2 oz) cointreau
60 mL (2 oz) brandy
375 mL (1-1/2 cups) soda water
24 ice cubes

Method
— In a punch bowl, combine the wine, sugar, and lemon and orange slices; stir to dissolve the sugar.
— Add the other ingredients, except the ice cubes.
— Let stand for 20 minutes.
— Add the ice cubes before serving.

* Marinate for 20 minutes before serving.

Christmas Punch*

Ingredients
2 L (8 cups) orange juice
175 mL (3/4 cup) lemon juice
250 mL (1 cup) brown sugar
750 mL (26 oz) gin
12 slices orange
3 slices fresh pineapple
125 mL (1/2 cup) grenadine syrup
750 mL (26 oz) bottle ginger beer
15 ice cubes
whole cherries, to taste

Method
— In a large bowl, combine the fruit juices, brown sugar, gin, slices of fruit and grenadine syrup; marinate for 12 hours.
— Add the ginger beer, ice cubes and cherries before serving.

* Marinate for 12 hours before serving.

A Delicious New Year

Whether you are celebrating the end of the old year or the beginning of the new one, December 31 is always a festive day, usually spent with a large number of guests. Surrounded by streamers and crackers, listening to music or dancing, everyone is waiting for the stroke of midnight to announce the beginning of an exciting new year.

The table is loaded with food and is as festive as the atmosphere. With the whole family there, from Aunt Agnes to that little rascal Billy, or with the whole gang of friends, there are often organizational problems in the kitchen.

These problems are complicated because of New Year's, the party usually goes on until the small hours of the morning. Guests arrive all night long; some just drop in for a moment while others stay all night. To keep all these people happy, lots of little appetizers are needed as well as a combination of heartier dishes for a balanced meal. Plan on preparing both cold and hot platters and balancing starch, meat and vegetable dishes.

Most recipes are planned for no more than 8 servings, except of course for the gigantic holiday turkey. If you are expecting more people, don't double the recipe; prepare, instead, different kinds of appetizers. For inspiration, consult *Appetizers,* Volume 15, of Microwave Magic.

Celebrate the beginning of the year with a successful party.

From the Recipe to Your Table

Unfortunately, no party prepares itself. Planning a meal for a number of friends or relatives is hard work and takes organization. Cooking a complete meal in the microwave oven must be planned ahead in the same way as a meal cooked in a conventional oven. Only the cooking and reheating times vary.

The night before the meal:
—Prepare the stuffed bread and the aspic. Cook the cake, cover with syrup and refrigerate.
The morning of the meal:
—Cook the stuffing and decorate the cake.
3 hours 20 minutes before the meal:
—Cook the turkey.
20 minutes before the meal:
—Cook the carrots.
5 minutes before the meal:
—Reheat the stuffed bread.

Stuffed Bread

Level of Difficulty	🍴🍴
Preparation Time	30 min*
Cost per Serving	$
Number of Servings	8
Nutritional Value	602 calories 28.5 g protein 37.6 g lipids
Food Exchanges	1 oz meat 2 bread exchanges 1 milk exchange 5-1/2 fat exchanges
Cooking Time	38 min
Standing Time	None
Power Level	100%, 50%
Write Your Cooking Time Here	

* Prepare 1 day ahead.

Ingredients
1 loaf of bread, 30 cm (12 in) long
450 g (1 lb) bacon
225 g (8 oz) ground veal
1 large Spanish onion, finely chopped
1 clove garlic, crushed
125 mL (1/2 cup) fresh parsley, chopped
50 mL (1/4 cup) celery leaves, chopped
6 small potatoes
75 mL (1/3 cup) hot water
hot chicken bouillon
savory to taste
salt and pepper to taste
2 284 mL (10 oz) cans cream of chicken soup
250 mL (1 cup) milk

Method
— Cut one thick slice from one end of the loaf of bread; set aside.
— Remove the inside of the loaf, leaving 1.5 cm (1/2 in) of bread around the sides; set aside the scooped out bread.
— Put 6 slices of bacon on a bacon tray and cook at 100% for 4 to 6 minutes; repeat until all the bacon is cooked; set aside 45 mL (3 tablespoons) of bacon fat.
— Put the onion and garlic in a dish and add some of the bacon fat; cover and cook at 100% for 3 minutes, stirring once during the cooking time.
— Add the parsley and celery, cover and continue cooking at 100% for 2 minutes, stirring once during the cooking time.
— Add the veal and cook at 100% for 4 to 5 minutes; stir and break up the meat twice during the cooking time.
— Add the crumbled bacon;

set the mixture aside and let cool.
— Peel the potatoes and cube them; put them in a dish and add the hot water.
— Cook at 100% for 9 to 11 minutes, stirring once after 5 minutes.
— Whip the potatoes with a potato masher while gradually adding enough hot chicken bouillon to bind them together.
— Combine the potatoes with the meat mixture; season with savory, salt and pepper.
— Fill the bread cavity with the stuffing, packing it in well.
— Replace the reserved end piece of bread and attach it to the loaf with toothpicks.
— Cover the bread with aluminum foil and refrigerate.
— Remove the bread from the refrigerator 1 hour before serving; keep it wrapped up.
— To prepare the sauce, combine the cream of chicken soup with the milk, heat at 100% for 4 to 6 minutes, beating with a whisk every 2 minutes.
— Unwrap the bread and cover it with paper towel; heat at 50% for 3 to 5 minutes, giving the dish a half-turn after 2 minutes.
— Slice the bread and serve it with the sauce.

Delicious Aspic

Level of Difficulty	
Preparation Time	20 min
Cost per Serving	$
Number of Servings	8
Nutritional Value	66 calories 16.2 g carbohydrate
Food Exchanges	1 fruit exchange
Cooking Time	3 min
Standing Time	None
Power Level	100%
Write Your Cooking Time Here	

Ingredients
1 package powdered
lemon-flavored gelatin
175 mL (3/4 cup) water
30 mL (2 tablespoons) lemon
juice
250 mL (1 cup) pineapple
juice
175 mL (3/4 cup) pineapple,
in pieces
250 mL (1 cup) carrots,
grated
watercress, to taste

Method
— Pour water into a bowl
  and heat at 100% for 3
  minutes.
— Add the flavored gelatin
  and stir to dissolve.
— Add the lemon and
  pineapple juices.
— Refrigerate until the
  mixture is half set.
— Stir in the pineapple and
  carrots; set aside.
— Rinse 8 ramekins in cold
  water; pour in the aspic.
— Refrigerate until the
  mixture is completely set.
— Arrange some watercress
  on a serving platter and
  unmold the ramekins on
  top.

*A delicious aspic will enhance
any holiday menu; assemble
these few ingredients and make
the aspic in less than 30
minutes.*

Dissolve the flavored gelatin in hot water, then add the lemon and pineapple juices.

Add the pineapple and carrots to the partially set aspic.

MICROTIPS

Aspics: for More Variety

Aspics are made from molded gelatin, juices, and fruits and vegetables. They are as delicious as they are decorative. The recipe we suggest here uses a fruit and vegetable mixture. Aspics can also be made with meat, seafood, fish, etc.

23

Holiday Turkey

Level of Difficulty	🍴
Preparation Time	40 min
Cost per Serving	$ $
Number of Servings	20
Nutritional Value	811 calories 64.3 g protein 4.2 mg iron
Food Exchanges	6 oz meat 7 fat exchanges
Cooking Time	3 h 16 min
Standing Time	10 min
Power Level	100%, 70%
Write Your Cooking Time Here	

Ingredients
1 turkey, 5.4 kg (12 lb)
125 mL (1/2 cup) softened butter
30 mL (2 tablespoons) mustard
45 mL (3 tablespoons) flour
1 large cooking bag

Stuffing:
50 mL (1/4 cup) butter
500 mL (2 cups) Spanish onion, chopped
2 cloves garlic, crushed
375 mL (1-1/2 cups) celery, chopped
125 mL (1/2 cup) celery leaves, chopped
125 mL (1/2 cup) fresh parsley, chopped
675 g (1-1/2 lb) ground veal
675 g (1-1/2 lb) ground pork

250 to 500 mL (1 to 2 cups) cooked mashed potatoes
salt and pepper to taste
poultry spices and savory to taste

Method
— To prepare the stuffing, combine the butter, Spanish onion, garlic, celery, celery leaves and parsley in a dish; cover and cook at 100% for 3 to 4 minutes, stirring once during the cooking time; set aside.
— Put the veal and pork into another dish and cook, uncovered, at 100% for 9 to 12 minutes, stirring and breaking up the meat

⇒

Holiday Turkey

Combine these ingredients to prepare turkey, a popular, traditional dish.

Cook the onion, garlic, celery, celery leaves and parsley in the butter.

Remove as much fat as possible and discard; add the vegetables and mix well.

Add enough mashed potatoes to thicken the mixture. Season to taste and let cool.

Fill the turkey with the stuffing; do not pack it in too tightly. Leave room for it to expand during cooking.

Turn the turkey over every 30 minutes to ensure uniform cooking.

every 3 minutes.
— Remove as much fat as possible and discard; add the vegetables and mixed well.
— Add enough mashed potatoes to thicken the mixture; season.
— Let cool.
— Stuff the turkey; truss it and sew up the opening

with string.
— In a small bowl, combine the butter, mustard and flour; brush the turkey with this mixture and put it into the cooking bag.
— Put the turkey in a dish and close the bag, leaving a small opening for steam to escape.
— Cook at 70% for 2-1/2 to

3 hours, or until the turkey is cooked, turning it over every 30 minutes.
— Let stand for 10 minutes.
— Remove the turkey from the bag and skim off as much fat as possible from the cooking juices; strain the juices through a sieve.
— Serve the turkey with its sauce.

Vichy Carrots

Ingredients
900 g (2 lb) carrots, cut in thin coins
75 mL (1/3 cup) butter
50 mL (1/4 cup) Vichy-

Célestins mineral water
5 mL (1 teaspoon) sugar
2 mL (1/2 teaspoon) thyme
salt and pepper to taste

Method
— Combine all the ingredients, except the salt and pepper, in a dish.
— Cover and cook at 100% for 9 to 12 minutes, stirring once during the cooking time.
— Let stand for 3 minutes.
— Remove the carrots from the dish and drain; season before serving.

Level of Difficulty	🍴
Preparation Time	20 min
Cost per Serving	$
Number of Servings	8
Nutritional Value	115 calories 12 g glucids 12.8 I.U. Vitamin A
Food Exchanges	3 vegetable exchanges 1 fat exchange
Cooking Time	12 min
Standing Time	3 min
Power Level	100%
Write Your Cooking Time Here	

Black Forest Cake

Level of Difficulty	🍴
Preparation Time	20 min*
Cost per Serving	$ $
Number of Servings	10
Nutritional Value	593 calories 52.7 g protein 7.5 g lipids
Food Exchanges	6 oz meat 1 bread exchange
Cooking Time	18 min
Standing Time	15 min
Power Level	100%, 70%
Write Your Cooking Time Here	

* Let the cake cool before decorating it.

Ingredients
150 mL (2/3 cup) butter
6 eggs
5 mL (1 teaspoon) vanilla
250 mL (1 cup) sugar
125 mL (1/2 cup) flour
125 mL (1/2 cup) cocoa

Syrup:
175 mL (3/4 cup) sugar
250 mL (1 cup) water
75 mL (1/3 cup) kirsch

Garnish:
540 mL (19 oz) can cherry
pie filling
750 mL (3 cups) 35% cream,
whipped
dark chocolate shavings and
maraschino cherries to
garnish

Method
— Put the butter in a dish
and heat at 100% for 2
minutes until melted;
skim off the foam and set
aside.
— In a bowl, combine the
eggs, vanilla and sugar
and beat at high speed
with an electric mixer for
10 minutes.
— Sift the flour and cocoa,
and gradually add to the
egg mixture.
— Add the butter and mix
until smooth.
— Grease 3 20 cm (8 in)
circular pans.
— Pour an equal amount of
batter into each pan.
— Cook one pan at a time;
put the pan on a raised
rack in the oven and
cook at 70% for 3
minutes, giving the dish a
half-turn after 2 minutes;
set the power level to
100% and continue
cooking for 1 minute.
— Cover the pan and let
stand for 5 minutes.
— Repeat this procedure

with the other two pans.
— Let cool completely
  before turning out.
— To prepare the syrup,
  combine the sugar and
  water in a dish; heat at
  100% for 3 to 4 minutes
  and stir to dissolve the
  sugar.
— Let cool and add the
  kirsch; mix well.
— Pour an equal amount of
  syrup over each cake
  letting it soak in.
— Spread half the cherry pie

filling on top of one
cake.
— Lay another cake over
  the cherry garnish and
  spread the remaining
  garnish on top.
— Add the last layer of
  cake.
— Spread whipped cream
  over the top and sides of
  the cake.
— Garnish with dark
  chocolate shavings and
  the maraschino cherries.

*All your guests will enjoy this
delicious cake. First assemble
all the ingredients required.*

Valentine's Day Delights

If cupids could depend on their magic arrows to make a young girl fall in love with a gallant young man, today's lovers can also use many romantic resources . . .

Valentine's Day is a holiday for lovers, a day to celebrate by enjoying candlelight supper. The romantic mood is set with lace and heart decorations in pink and red, the colors traditionally associated with love and passion. Usually, it's dinner for two on the 14th of February. Is there anything nicer than sharing a romantic supper with a loved one?

This is one occasion when you will really appreciate the advantages of a microwave oven. There is nothing less romantic than greeting your Valentine in a messy kitchen while you are trying to finish the preparations. The microwave oven lets you do most of the work ahead of time.

For the menu, choose delicate dishes to be slowly savored as you linger over the meal. Add a light note to this very special evening by serving an aspic or a salad prepared in a heart-shaped mold. For dessert, enjoy a sweet treat. After all this is one occasion that can never be too sweet.

From the Recipe to Your Table
Unfortunately, no party prepares itself. Planning a meal for a number of friends or relatives is hard work and takes organization. Cooking a complete meal in the microwave oven must be planned ahead in the same way as a meal cooked in a microwave oven. Only the cooking and reheating times vary.

The morning of the meal:
—Prepare the soup. Make the Grand Marnier sauce and prepare the fruit cups.
1 hour before the meal:
—Prepare the rice.
30 minutes before the meal:
—Cook the salmon.
5 minutes before the meal:
—Pour the sauce into the fruit cups.

Curried Apple Soup*

Level of Difficulty	🍴
Preparation Time	15 min
Cost per Serving	**$**
Number of Servings	8
Nutritional Value	76 calories 10.1 g carbohydrate 3.8 g lipids
Food Exchanges	1 fruit exchange 1/2 fat exchange
Cooking Time	None
Standing Time	None
Power Level	None
Write Your Cooking Time Here	✏️🍎

* Refrigerate for 2 hours before serving.

Ingredients
380 mL (13 oz) apple juice
5 mL (1 teaspoon) curry
250 mL (1 cup) applesauce
15 mL (1 tablespoon) grated onion
125 mL (1/2 cup) 15% cream
15 mL (1 tablespoon) fresh parsley, chopped
15 green olives, pitted and chopped
300 mL (1-1/4 cups) water
30 mL (2 tablespoons) chicken bouillon

Method
— In a large bowl combine all the ingredients.
— Pour the mixture into a blender and purée for a few seconds until smooth.
— Refrigerate for 2 hours before serving.

This exquisite soup is easy to make. These are the ingredients you will need.

Pour the mixture into a blender and purée for a few seconds until smooth, then refrigerate for 2 hours.

MICROTIPS

For a Tastier Compote

Fruits tend to get overcooked when used to prepare a compote. When you taste a perfectly cooked compote you notice the difference. A good compote is made from many pieces of fruit which melt in your mouth and taste delicious. You can identify an overcooked compote by its texture, which resembles mashed potatoes, and by its overly sweet taste. Always consider the firmness of the fruits used before deciding the cooking time and carefully avoid overcooking.

Salmon with Armagnac

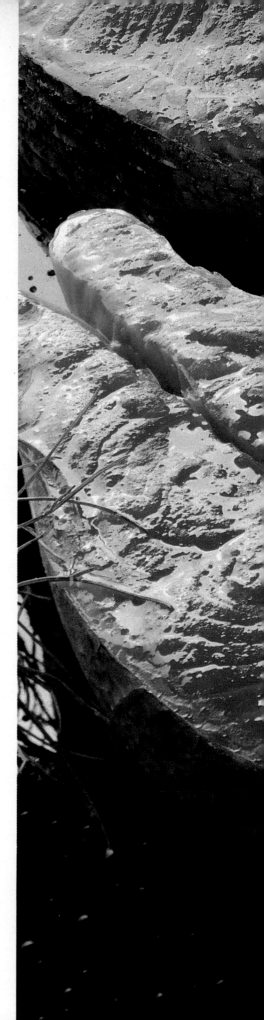

Level of Difficulty	🍴🔪
Preparation Time	10 min
Cost per Serving	$ $
Number of Servings	8
Nutritional Value	387 calories 34 g protein 15.3 g lipids
Food Exchanges	5 oz meat 1/2 fat exchange
Cooking Time	30 min
Standing Time	5 min
Power Level	70%
Write Your Cooking Time Here	

Ingredients
8 salmon steaks, 175 g (6 oz) each
2 onions, sliced
2 lemons, sliced
salt and pepper to taste
paprika to taste
parsley to taste
50 mL (1/4 cup) butter
250 mL (1 cup) armagnac

Method
— Spread the onion and lemon slices on the bottom of a large dish.
— Salt and pepper the salmon steaks and place in the dish; sprinkle with paprika and parsley and dot with small pieces of butter.

⇒

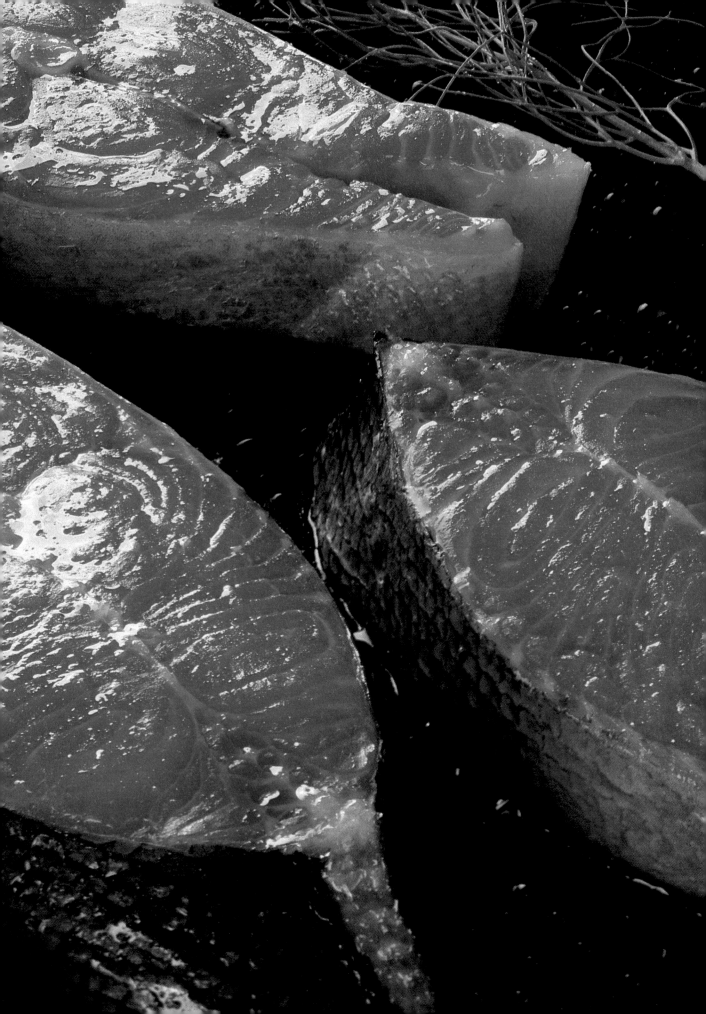

Salmon with Armagnac

Spread the onion and lemon slices on the bottom of a large dish.

Salt and pepper the steaks.

Put the steaks in the dish; sprinkle with paprika and parsley.

Dot with pieces of butter, cover and begin cooking.

Give the dish a half-turn and turn the steaks over after the first stage of cooking.

Let stand, covered, for 5 minutes before serving.

— Cover the dish and cook at 70% for 15 minutes.
— Give the dish a half-turn and turn the steaks over.
— Cover and continue

cooking at 70% for 10 minutes.
— Sprinkle with armagnac and cover; continue cooking at 70% for 5

minutes, or until the steaks are cooked.
— Let stand, covered, for 5 minutes.

Rice Pilaf

Ingredients

500 mL (2 cups) long grain rice
50 mL (1/4 cup) butter

925 mL (3-3/4 cups) hot chicken bouillon
125 mL (1/2 cup) celery, diced

125 mL (1/2 cup) green onions, chopped
50 mL (1/4 cup) soy sauce
150 mL (2/3 cup) mushrooms, thinly sliced

Level of Difficulty	🍴
Preparation Time	20 min
Cost per Serving	**$**
Number of Servings	8
Nutritional Value	147 calories 19.5 g carbohydrate 5.8 g lipids
Food Exchanges	1 vegetable exchange 1 bread exchange 1 fat exchange
Cooking Time	26 min
Standing Time	10 min
Power Level	100%, 70%
Write Your Cooking Time Here	

Method

— Combine the rice and butter in a dish; cook uncovered at 100% for 4 to 5 minutes, stirring twice during the cooking time.
— Add all the other ingredients, except the mushrooms.
— Cover and cook at 100% for 10 minutes.
— Stir and cover the dish; continue cooking at 70% for 9 to 11 minutes.
— Add the mushrooms and cover the dish.
— Let stand for 10 minutes.

Fruit Cup with Grand Marnier

Level of Difficulty	🍴🍴
Preparation Time	20 min*
Cost per Serving	$ $
Number of Servings	8
Nutritional Value	421 calories 40.6 g carbohydrate 25.6 g lipids
Food Exchanges	3 fruit exchanges 5 fat exchanges
Cooking Time	None
Standing Time	None
Power Level	None
Write Your Cooking Time Here	

* Let the sauce cool before serving.

Ingredients
1 L (4 cups) fruits (peaches, strawberries, pears, oranges, kiwi, etc.)
12 marshmallows
8 egg yolks
150 mL (2/3 cup) sugar
125 mL (1/2 cup) butter, melted
125 mL (1/2 cup) fruit juice, to taste
50 mL (1/4 cup) Grand Marnier
500 mL (2 cups) 35% cream
8 cherries

Method
— Cut the fruits and marshmallows into pieces; put them in 8 small cups and set aside.
— In a bowl, beat the egg yolks until thick and lemon-colored.
— Gradually add in the following order, the sugar, melted butter, fruit juice and the Grand Marnier; set aside.
— Whip the cream and fold half into the sauce; chill, reserving the remaining whipped cream until ready to serve.
— Pour the sauce over the fruit; garnish with the reserved whipped cream and cherry.

This scrumptious dessert will be a treat for all your guests. These are the ingredients required.

Beat the egg yolks until thick and lemon-colored.

Stirring vigorously, add first the sugar, then the butter. Then blend in the fruit juice and the Grand Marnier.

Easter Treats

Easter is the time to celebrate the renewal of life. It's a religious holiday that coincides with the return of spring and the first warm rays of the sun. All around us nature is reborn; snow disappears, baby birds appear in nests, lawns turn green again and woolens are packed away in cedar chests.

Wonderful childhood memories relate to Easter, that spring Sunday when, every year, a mysterious bunny leaves a straw basket full of goodies beside the bed. Morning signals the beginning of a treasure hunt for chocolate and decorated eggs hidden throughout the house.

To celebrate the return of good weather, fresh vegetables, plain or in salads, are the centerpiece of the Easter menu. Green, crispy and full of life, they give a foretaste of good things to come. And to really celebrate the new season, leave the windows open during the meal!

From the Recipe to Your Table

Unfortunately, no meal prepares itself. Planning a meal for a number of friends or relatives is hard work and takes organization. Cooking a complete meal in the microwave oven must be planned ahead in the same way as a meal cooked in a conventional oven. Only the cooking and reheating times vary.

The night before the meal:
—Prepare the fruit pizza.
The morning of the meal:
—Prepare the salad dressing.
2 hours 30 minutes before the meal:
—Cook the pork roast.
20 minutes before the meal:
—Cook the ham and broccoli rolls.
5 minutes before the meal:
—Cook the fiddleheads and finish preparing the salad.

Green Salad

Level of Difficulty	🍴
Preparation Time	15 min*
Cost per Serving	$
Number of Servings	10
Nutritional Value	112 calories 9.6 g lipids
Food Exchanges	2 fat exchanges 1 vegetable exchange
Cooking Time	6 min
Standing Time	None
Power Level	100%
Write Your Cooking Time Here	

* Refrigerate the vinaigrette before serving.

Ingredients
1 large leafy lettuce
30 mL (2 tablespoons) cornstarch
500 mL (2 cups) water
20 mL (4 teaspoons) juice from marinated pickles
125 mL (1/2 cup) mayonnaise
20 mL (4 teaspoons) mustard
3 drops Tabasco sauce
3 drops Worcestershire sauce
1 mL (1/4 teaspoon) horseradish
30 mL (2 tablespoons) beef bouillon concentrate

Method
— Rinse the lettuce in cold water and dry; tear into bite-size pieces; set aside.
— Combine the cornstarch and water, and heat at 100% for 5 to 6 minutes, stirring every 2 minutes.
— Combine the remaining ingredients and whisk until creamy.
— Combine the 2 mixtures and whisk again until smooth; let cool.
— Pour the vinaigrette over the lettuce and toss before serving.

This delicious green salad will add a fresh note to your Easter menu.

42

Combine the cornstarch and water, then heat at 100% for 5 to 6 minutes.

Combine the 2 mixtures and whisk until smooth.

MICROTIPS

Peeling Tomatoes
To peel tomatoes easily first blanch them in the microwave oven. To do this, half fill a casserole with water. Cover and bring the water to a boil. Plunge the tomatoes into the boiling water for just a few seconds; drain and then plunge them into cold water. The skins will slip off easily.

43

Broccoli and Ham Rolls

Level of Difficulty	
Preparation Time	30 min
Cost per Serving	$
Number of Servings	10
Nutritional Value	185 calories 10.9 g protein 12.4 g lipids
Food Exchanges	1.5 oz meat 1 vegetable exchange 1 fat exchange
Cooking Time	18 min
Standing Time	3 min
Power Level	100%, 70%
Write Your Cooking Time Here	

Ingredients
10 slices cooked ham
20 broccoli flowerets
50 mL (1/4 cup) water
1 284 mL (10 oz) can cream of mushroom soup
75 mL (1/3 cup) milk
50 mL (1/4 cup) mayonnaise
50 mL (1/4 cup) dry white wine
125 mL (1/2 cup) mushrooms, chopped
150 mL (2/3 cup) Parmesan cheese, grated
paprika to taste

Method
— In a bowl, combine the cream of mushroom soup, milk, mayonnaise, white wine and mushrooms.
— Spread some of the sauce over the slices of ham to lightly cover them; roll up the slices and arrange in a dish; reserve the remaining sauce.
— Put the broccoli flowerets in a dish and add water; cover and cook at 100% for 5 to 7 minutes, stirring once halfway through the cooking time. Drain and refresh under running cold water.
— Garnish each end of the rolled ham slices with a broccoli flowerets; cover with the remaining sauce and sprinkle with the Parmesan cheese and paprika.
— Cook at 70% for 9 to 11 minutes, giving the dish a half-turn after 5 minutes.
— Let stand for 3 minutes before serving.

These delicious ham rolls can be made in less than an hour. First assemble the ingredients required.

Spread part of the sauce over the ham slices to lightly cover them, then roll them up.

Only use the tops of the broccoli. Cook them in a covered dish with a small amount of water at 100% for 5 to 7 minutes. Stir halfway through the cooking time.

Roast Pork

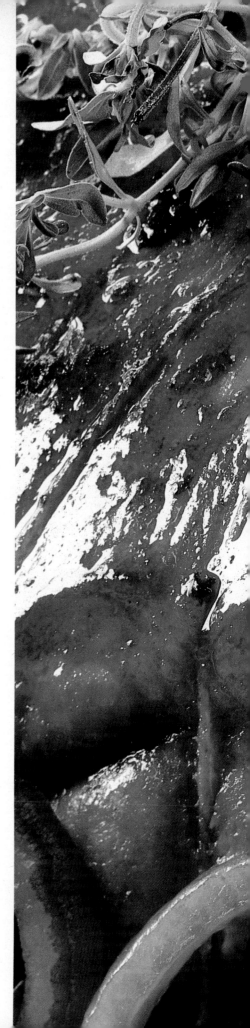

Level of Difficulty	🍴🍴
Preparation Time	20 min*
Cost per Serving	$ $
Number of Servings	10
Nutritional Value	593 calories 52.7 g protein 7.5 mg iron
Food Exchanges	6 oz meat 1 vegetable exchange 1 bread exchange 1 fat exchange
Cooking Time	1 h 24 min
Standing Time	None
Power Level	100%, 50%
Write Your Cooking Time Here	

* The roast is set aside for 30 minutes to allow the garlic to flavor the meat.

Ingredients
1 rolled pork roast, 2.25 kg (5 lb)
4 cloves garlic, cut in slivers
75 mL (1/3 cup) butter
6 red onions, sliced
125 mL (1/2 cup) undiluted beef consommé
pepper to taste
10 potatoes, peeled and thinly sliced

Method
— With a small sharp knife, make several small cuts in the roast and insert the slivers of garlic; set aside for 30 minutes at room temperature.
— Preheat a browning dish at 100% for 7 minutes; add the butter and heat at 100% for 30 seconds.
— Sear the roast on all sides and remove it from the pan.
— Spread the onion slices on the bottom of the dish and place the roast on top of them.
— Pour the consommé over the roast and season with pepper.

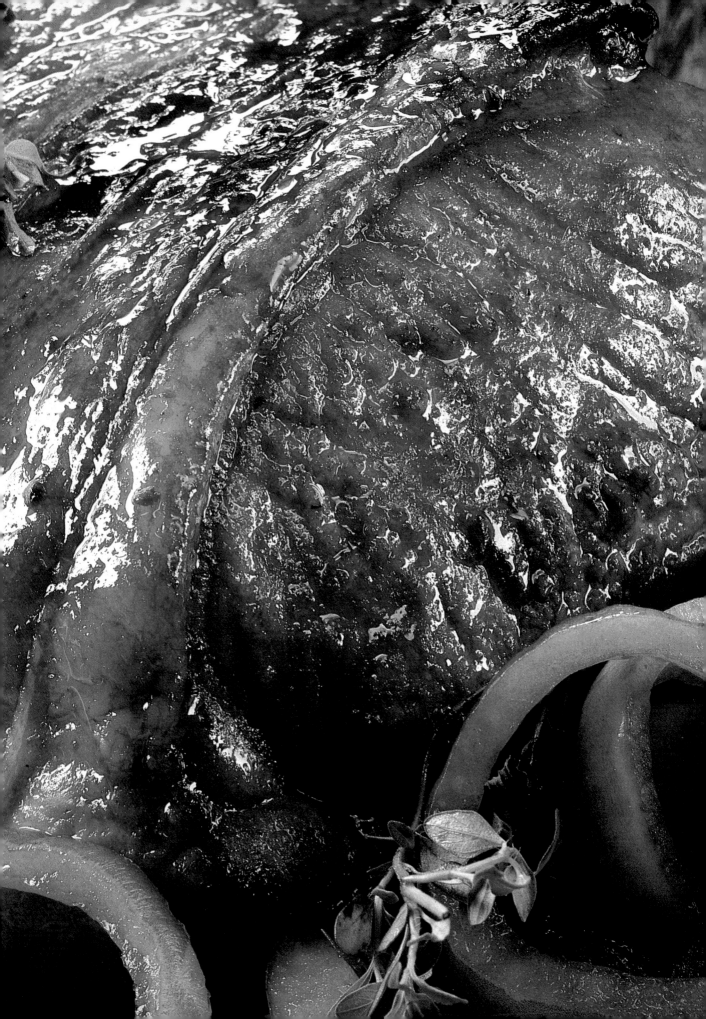

Roast Pork

This traditional roast is always appreciated. First assemble the required ingredients.

Sear the roast in the preheated baking dish containing butter.

Spread the onions in the bottom of the dish, before adding the roast.

Turn the roast over between the first two stages of cooking.

Cover the cooked parts of the roast with aluminum foil, before beginning the last stage of cooking.

When the roast is cooked, remove it and cover it with aluminum foil, shiny side against the meat to keep it warm.

— Cover and cook at 50% for 40 seconds. Return the roast to the dish.
— Cover and continue cooking at 50% for 40 minutes.
— Turn the roast over.
— Cover the cooked parts of the roast and the ends with aluminum foil.
— Cover and continue

cooking at 50% for 20 to 30 minutes, or until the roast is tender.
— Remove the roast and cover it with aluminum foil, shiny side toward the meat; keep it warm.
— Add the potatoes to the cooking juices.
— Cover and cook at 100% for 10 to 13 minutes,

stirring once during the cooking time.
— Remove the aluminum foil from the roast and carve it.
— Skim as much fat as possible from the liquid in the pan. Serve the roast accompanied by the potatoes.

Fiddleheads

Ingredients
1.25 L (5 cups) frozen
fiddleheads
50 mL (1/4 cup) lemon juice
50 mL (1/4 cup) butter

Method
— Put the fiddleheads in a
dish, add the lemon juice
and butter.
— Cover and cook at 100%

for 4 to 6 minutes,
stirring lightly halfway
through the cooking time.
— Let stand for 3 minutes
before serving.

Level of Difficulty	🍴
Preparation Time	5 min
Cost per Serving	$
Number of Servings	10
Nutritional Value	62 calories 4.9 g lipids
Food Exchanges	1 vegetable exchange 1 fat exchange
Cooking Time	6 min
Standing Time	3 min
Power Level	100%
Write Your Cooking Time Here	🍎✏️

Fruit Pizza

Level of Difficulty	¶¶
Preparation Time	35 min*
Cost per Serving	$ $
Number of Servings	8
Nutritional Value	342 calories 7.4 g protein 64.8 g carbohydrate
Food Exchanges	3 fruit exchanges 1 bread exchange 1/2 fat exchange
Cooking Time	18 min
Standing Time	None
Power Level	100%, 50%
Write Your Cooking Time Here	

* Cool the dough before garnishing it.

Ingredients
2 eggs
250 mL (1 cup) sugar
15 mL (1 tablespoon) butter
250 mL (1 cup) flour
1 pinch salt
5 mL (1 teaspoon) baking powder
125 mL (1/2 cup) milk
fruits, such as strawberries, grapes, raspberries, melon balls

Pastry Cream:
500 mL (2 cups) milk
1 pinch salt
4 drops vanilla
2 eggs
75 mL (1/3 cup) cornstarch
175 mL (3/4 cup) sugar

Sauce:
125 mL (1/2 cup) fruit juice
30 mL (2 tablespoons) flour

Method
— To prepare the pastry cream, combine the milk, salt and vanilla in a bowl and mix.
— Cook at 100% for 5 minutes, stirring twice during the cooking time; set aside.
— In a bowl, beat the eggs; gradually add the cornstarch and sugar; add to the milk mixture and beat well.
— Cook at 100% for 2 to 3 minutes, stirring twice.
— Lay a piece of plastic wrap directly on the surface; set aside.
— To prepare the dough, combine the eggs, sugar and butter, and beat until smooth; set aside.
— Sift the flour, salt and baking powder. Add to the egg mixture alternately with the milk; begin and end with the

dry ingredients.
— Transfer the mixture to a large pizza plate.
— Put the plate on a raised rack in the oven and cook at 50% for 6 to 8 minutes; let cool.
— Pour in the pastry cream and garnish with fruits.
— Combine the sauce ingredients; cook at 100% for 2 minutes, stirring twice.
— Brush the sauce on top before serving.

To save time and fuss, assemble the ingredients before beginning to prepare this colorful dessert.

Brush the top of the fruit with the sauce before serving.

Mother's Day Celebration

While cooking is certainly a fascinating pastime, kitchen work often falls on mothers and this pastime quickly loses its charm. Many moms would rather be doing other things instead of being tied to the stove for long hours at a time.

Once a year fortunately, mothers are chased from the kitchen. On Mother's Day, they deserve to relax and be waited on by other members of the family.

Very often, just before the first meal on Mother's Day, whispers and giggles can be heard in the kitchen, where the children are secretly preparing breakfast in bed for mother, who pretends to be fast asleep. And it's hard to say whether it's mother or child, who will be happiest when a pretty tray with delicious food and spring flowers arrives in the bedroom!

The microwave oven is ideal for children who want to prepare omelettes and other egg dishes. They can also heat buns, fry bacon without making a mess and even prepare coffee. It is perfectly safe to let the children help with such items since neither the oven nor the dishes become hot enough to cause harm. Older children can even prepare full meals, with father's help.

Served with a pretty card, the menu for Mother's Day will create many happy memories for mother! A last word: Mother's Day will only be a complete success if Sunday cooks are careful to clean up the kitchen after displaying their talents . . . .

From the Recipe to Your Table

Unfortunately, no meal prepares itself. Planning a meal for a number of friends or family is hard work and takes organization. Cooking a complete meal in the microwave oven must be planned ahead in the same way as a meal cooked in a conventional oven. Only the cooking and reheating times vary.

The night before the meal:
—Marinate the rabbit. Cook the vegetables and prepare the cake.
The morning of the meal:
—Prepare the eggs.
2 hours before the meal:
—Prepare and cook the rabbit.

Antilles Eggs

Level of Difficulty	🍴🍴 🍴🍴
Preparation Time	30 min*
Cost per Serving	$ $
Number of Servings	10
Nutritional Value	302 calories 14.2 g protein 2.1 mg iron
Food Exchanges	2 oz meat 1 fruit exchange 2 fat exchanges
Cooking Time	None
Standing Time	None
Power Level	None
Write Your Cooking Time Here	

* Soak the anchovy fillets for 1 hour before preparing the recipe.

Ingredients
10 hard-cooked eggs
6 flat anchovy fillets, salted
20 thin slices pineapple
1 284 g (10 oz) can tuna
45 mL (3 tablespoons) capers
90 g (3 oz) black olives, pitted and chopped
90 mL (6 tablespoons) olive oil
30 mL (2 tablespoons) lemon juice
45 mL (3 tablespoons) rum
1 pinch cayenne
pepper to taste

Method
— Cover the anchovies with cold water and soak for 1 hour to desalt.
— Shell the eggs, cut them in half lengthwise and remove the yolks; set the yolks aside.
— Put one half egg white on each slice of pineapple; refrigerate.
— In a bowl, mash the egg yolks, tuna, capers and black olives; pat the anchovies dry and add to the mixture.
— Transfer to a blender and purée for a few seconds until smooth.
— Season with cayenne and pepper to taste.
— Stuff the egg halves with the egg yolk and tuna mixture and serve.

These delicious hors d'oeuvres will be a hit with your guests. These are the ingredients required to prepare them.

Put one half egg white on each slice of pineapple and refrigerate. In the meantime, prepare the stuffing.

Stuff the egg halves with the egg yolk and tuna mixture and serve.

Rabbit with Mustard

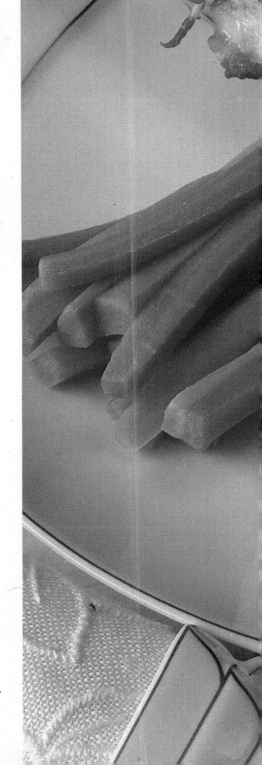

Level of Difficulty	🍴🍴
Preparation Time	20 min*
Cost per Serving	$ $
Number of Servings	8
Nutritional Value	515 calories 55.5 g protein 17.8 g lipids
Food Exchanges	6 oz meat 2 fat exchanges
Cooking Time	1 h 14 min
Standing Time	None
Power Level	100%, 70%
Write Your Cooking Time Here	

* Refrigerate the rabbits for 24 hours before cooking.

Ingredients
2 rabbits, 1.8 kg (4 lb) each
75 mL (1/3 cup) Dijon mustard
125 mL (1/2 cup) butter
250 mL (1 cup) dry white wine
250 mL (1 cup) 35% cream

Method
— Brush the rabbits with the Dijon mustard and refrigerate for 24 hours.
— Preheat a browning dish at 100% for 7 minutes, add 50 mL (1/4 cup) of the butter and heat at 100% for 30 seconds.
— Sear one of the rabbits and remove.
— Heat the browning dish at 100% for 5 minutes, add the remaining butter, sear the other rabbit and remove.
— Pour the wine into the dish and scrape up the little bits that cling to the bottom and sides.

⟹

Rabbit with Mustard

Dijon mustard, butter, white wine and 35% cream are the only ingredients needed to make this delicious rabbit recipe.

Brush the rabbits with mustard and refrigerate for 24 hours.

Sear the rabbits one at a time in a preheated browning dish.

Pour the wine into the dish and deglaze with a spatula.

To ensure even cooking, turn the rabbits over between the 2 stages of cooking.

Add the cream to the cooking juices and cook at 100% for 3 minutes to make the sauce.

— Return the rabbits to the dish, cover and cook at 70% for 30 minutes.
— Turn the rabbits over and cover the dish again; continue cooking at 70% for 30 to 40 minutes, or until the rabbits are cooked.
— Remove the rabbits and cover them with aluminum foil, shiny side against the meat; keep warm.
— Add the cream to the cooking juices and cook at 100% for 3 minutes, stirring twice during the cooking time; season to taste.
— Uncover the rabbits and serve with the sauce.

Marinated Vegetables

Ingredients

1 cauliflower, cut into flowerets
3 carrots, cut into sticks
2 celery stalks, cut into sticks

1 green pepper, cut into strips
125 mL (1/2 cup) stuffed olives
250 mL (1 cup) green beans

175 mL (3/4 cup) white wine vinegar
175 mL (3/4 cup) water
125 mL (1/2 cup) oil
30 mL (2 tablespoons) sugar
3 mL (3/4 teaspoon) oregano pepper

Method

— In a 4 L (16 cup) casserole, combine all the ingredients and mix well.
— Cover and cook at 100% for 5 minutes.
— Stir, cover the dish again and continue cooking at 100% for 5 minutes.
— Let cool and refrigerate for 24 hours, stirring several times.

Level of Difficulty	🍴🍴
Preparation Time	20 min*
Cost per Serving	$
Number of Servings	10
Nutritional Value	140 calories 7.6 g carbohydrate
Food Exchanges	2 vegetable exchanges 2 fat exchanges
Cooking Time	10 min
Standing Time	None
Power Level	100%
Write Your Cooking Time Here	

* Let the vegetables cool and then refrigerate them before serving.

Orange Crown Cake

Level of Difficulty	🍴
Preparation Time	30 min*
Cost per Serving	$
Number of Servings	10
Nutritional Value	393 calories 56 g carbohydrate
Food Exchanges	2 fruit exchanges 2 bread exchanges 2-1/2 fat exchanges
Cooking Time	6 min
Standing Time	None
Power Level	70%
Write Your Cooking Time Here	

* Cool before serving.

Ingredients
3 egg whites
3 egg yolks
75 mL (1/3 cup) orange juice
250 mL (1 cup) sugar
250 mL (1 cup) flour
1 mL (1/4 teaspoon) salt
5 mL (1 teaspoon) baking
powder

Frosting:
50 mL (1/4 cup) butter
213 mL (7.5 oz) package
cream cheese
500 to 625 mL (2 to
2-1/2 cups) icing sugar
125 mL (1/2 cup) grated
coconut
50 mL (1/4 cup) pecan pieces
5 mL (1 teaspoon) vanilla

Method
— Beat the egg whites to
stiff peaks with a whisk;
set aside.
— In a bowl, beat the egg
yolks, orange juice and
sugar; sift the flour, salt
and baking powder, and
gradually add to the egg
yolk mixture.
— Fold in the egg whites.
— Grease 2 L (8 cup) tube
pan and pour in the
batter.
— Place the pan on a raised
rack and cook at 70% for
4 to 6 minutes, giving the
pan a half-turn halfway
through the cooking time.
— Let cool.
— To prepare the frosting,
beat the butter and cream
cheese together.
— Slowly add the icing
sugar, then the coconut,
pecans and vanilla; stir
until smooth.
— Frost the cake before
serving.

This delicious dessert will satisfy the most demanding guest. These are the ingredients required to make the cake.

Beat the egg whites to stiff peaks with a whisk.

Grease a 2 L (8 cup) tube pan and pour in the batter.

A Menu for Father

During the summer, holidays are a good opportunity for the family to get together, to ride bicycles, play baseball or go for a swim. Our diet changes with the good weather; steaming soups and heaping plates of stews are no longer as attractive as they once were. However, Father's Day is not quite summer and a meat meal is still very pleasant. Here we would like to show you a delicious way of preparing a traditional roast beef. Served with a good Bordeaux or a Brouilly wine and with a first course of Mussels Bordelaise, this roast beef will be the main course of a meal that father will certainly enjoy.

Today's man is becoming more careful about his diet. On this final Sunday in spring, he will appreciate the vegetables and the light dessert planned for his Father's Day menu.

Finally, this day's meal would not be complete without some little surprises for the star of the day! So give your imagination free rein!

From the Recipe to Your Table

Unfortunately, no meal prepares itself. Planning a meal for a number of friends or family is hard work and takes organization. Cooking a complete meal in the microwave oven must be planned ahead in the same way as a meal cooked in a conventional oven. Only the cooking and reheating times vary.

The night before the meal:
—Prepare the Bourbon Mousse.
20 minutes before cooking the roast beef:
—Cook the mussels and prepare the sauce.
35 to 50 minutes before the meal:
—Cook the roast beef.
10 minutes before the meal:
—Cook the vegetables and reheat the mussels.

Mussels Bordelaise

Level of Difficulty	🍴
Preparation Time	20 min
Cost per Serving	$ $
Number of Servings	8
Nutritional Value	116 calories 4.4 g protein 6 g glucids
Food Exchanges	1 oz meat 2 fat exchanges
Cooking Time	18 min
Standing Time	None
Power Level	100%
Write Your Cooking Time Here	

Ingredients
1.3 kg (3 lb) mussels
75 mL (1/3 cup) water
1 onion, finely chopped
2 tomatoes, peeled, chopped and drained
125 mL (1/2 cup) butter
250 mL (1 cup) white wine
30 mL (2 tablespoons) dried parsley
1 bay leaf
2 mL (1/2 teaspoon) cayenne
salt to taste

Method
— Put the mussels in a dish and add the water; cover and cook at 100% for 5 to 7 minutes, or until the mussels have opened. Discard any that do not open.
— Drain the mussels; open the shells and remove the mussels; set aside.
— Combine the remaining ingredients in a casserole; cook at 100% for 5 minutes.
— Break up the tomatoes and continue cooking at 100% for 5 to 6 minutes.
— Return each mussel to half a shell and pour on the sauce before serving.

Assemble these ingredients to obtain a tantalizing first course of mussels which all your guests will enjoy.

Cook the mussels in a covered dish until they open.

Separate the shells and remove the mussels; set aside.

Break up the tomatoes between the first and second stages of cooking.

65

Roast Beef

Level of Difficulty	🍴🍴
Preparation Time	25 min
Cost per Serving	$ $
Number of Servings	6
Nutritional Value	356 calories 37.7 g protein 8.4 mg iron
Food Exchanges	3.5 oz meat 1/2 fat exchange
Cooking Time	11 to 17 min/kg (5 to 8 min/lb) + 2 min
Standing Time	10 min
Power Level	100%, 70%
Write Your Cooking Time Here	

Ingredients
1 rolled sirloin roast, 1.4 kg (3 lb)
50 mL (1/4 cup) butter
50 mL (1/4 cup) dry mustard
1 onion, sliced

Sauce:
2 cloves garlic, crushed
750 mL (3 cups) strong tea

Method
— Pepper the beef.
— Heat the butter at 100% for 30 seconds until melted.
— Add the mustard and mix well; brush over the beef.
— Cover with the onion slices.
— Put the beef into a dish and cook at 70% to taste:
very rare: 11 min/kg (5 min/lb);
rare: 13 min/kg (6 min/lb);
— medium: 15 min/kg (7 min/lb);
well-done: 17 min/kg (8 min/lb)
or using a temperature probe:

⇒

Roast Beef

Deglazing is a procedure used to make a sauce from the juices released during the cooking process.

To deglaze, pour a liquid (such as water, vinegar or a good white wine) into the dish used to cook the meat and add seasonings.

Use a wooden spoon or spatula to scrape the bits that cling to the bottom and sides of the pan. Heat and pour over the cooked meat before serving.

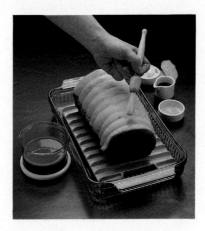

Brush the roast with the mixture of melted butter and mustard.

When the roast is cooked, cover it with aluminum foil and let stand for 10 minutes before serving.

very rare: 40°C (100°F);
rare: 45°C (110°F);
medium: 55°C (130°F);
well-done: 60°C (140°F).
— Remove the beef from the dish; cover with aluminum foil, shiny side against the meat.
— Let stand for 10 minutes.
— In the meantime, prepare the sauce: add the cloves of garlic and tea to the cooking juices; season to taste.
— With a spatula, scrape the bottom of the dish to deglaze it.
— Heat at 100% for 1 minute and scrape again; repeat this procedure until the sauce has thickened.

Note: To obtain a thicker sauce, add some cornstarch diluted in a small amount of cold water to the cooking juices before the last stage of cooking.

Mixed Vegetables

Ingredients
2 rutabagas
1 clove garlic, crushed
1 red pepper
1 green pepper

4 leeks, white part only
50 mL (1/4 cup) butter
30 mL (2 tablespoons) lemon juice
1 pinch nutmeg

15 mL (1 tablespoon) dried parsley
salt and pepper to taste

Method
— Cut the vegetables into julienne strips.
— Put the butter in a dish; add the rutabaga and garlic.
— Cover and cook at 100% for 2 minutes.
— Stir; add the peppers, leeks and lemon juice.
— Cover and cook at 100% for 4 to 6 minutes.
— Stir and add the remaining ingredients; season to taste.
— Cover and let stand for 2 minutes.

Level of Difficulty	🍴
Preparation Time	20 min
Cost per Serving	$
Number of Servings	8
Nutritional Value	70 calories 4.7 g carbohydrate 5.5 g lipids
Food Exchanges	1 vegetable exchange 1 fat exchange
Cooking Time	8 min
Standing Time	2 min
Power Level	100%
Write Your Cooking Time Here	

Bourbon Mousse

Level of Difficulty	🍴🍴
Preparation Time	20 min*
Cost per Serving	$ $
Number of Servings	6
Nutritional Value	180 calories 5.7 g carbohydrate 12.9 g lipids
Food Exchanges	1 fruit exchange 2-1/2 fat exchanges
Cooking Time	None
Standing Time	None
Power Level	None
Write Your Cooking Time Here	

* Freeze the mousse before serving.

Ingredients
3 egg whites
6 egg yolks
75 mL (1/3 cup) sugar
90 mL (3 oz) bourbon
250 mL (1 cup) 35% cream
butter
icing sugar
cocoa

Method
— Butter 6 small soufflé dishes.
— Place a strip of waxed paper inside each dish so that it sticks up 2.5 cm (1 in) over the top of the dish.
— Beat the egg whites to stiff peaks, gradually adding half the sugar.
— Beat the egg yolks, gradually adding the bourbon and remaining sugar.
— Whip the cream until thick.
— Combine the three mixtures.
— Quickly divide among the soufflé dishes.
— Freeze until set.
— Remove the waxed paper and sprinkle with a mixture of icing sugar and cocoa before serving.

To make this delicious dessert, first assemble these ingredients.

Place a strip of waxed paper inside each dish.

Combine the beaten egg whites, egg yolk mixture and cream.

Quickly pour an equal amount of the mixture into each dish and place in the freezer.

71

Halloween: A Mysterious Meal

On October 31, the eve of All Saints Day, it is thought that the dead come back to haunt us. That's the night for masked balls and costume parties. For young and old alike, the carved pumpkin with its frightening face is the symbol of Halloween. On this occasion, disguises, make-up and other accessories are the joy of children and it's fun, too, for grownups to join in and share their excitement by preparing a little party. To make sure that the party is a success, parents need to take care. Avoid disasters and disappointments by preparing simple meals for your young guests, meals which will not make a mess. Forget about exotic dishes and remember that children don't enjoy complicated culinary preparations with strange tastes. Finally, plan to use the microwave oven: you will really appreciate its speed since children are not usually very good at waiting.

The choice of recipes is vast since children will happily taste any dish, if it is presented in an amusing way. But just because Halloween is a holiday, that doesn't mean that nutritional foods and healthful treats should be struck from the menu. Make some homemade popcorn, for example (the microwave is ideal for that) and you will have happy faces all around you.

Your little guests will certainly gorge on the treats collected during their trips around the neighborhood. To prevent your children's teeth from being damaged by too much sugar, give them a small gift before they go to sleep: a good tooth brush! Traditions sometimes create obligations!

From the Recipe to Your Table

Unfortunately, no meal prepares itself. Planning a meal for a number of friends or relatives is hard work and takes organization. Cooking a complete meal in the microwave oven must be planned ahead in the same way as a meal cooked in a conventional oven. Only the cooking and reheating times vary.

Prepare everything but the veal the night before.

30 minutes before the meal:
—Cook the veal.

Cream of Carrot Soup*

Level of Difficulty	
Preparation Time	30 min
Cost per Serving	$
Number of Servings	12
Nutritional Value	112 calories 10.5 g glucids 8628 I.U. Vitamin A
Food Exchanges	2 vegetable exchanges 1-1/2 fat exchanges
Cooking Time	1 h 13 min
Standing Time	None
Power Level	100%, 70%
Write Your Cooking Time Here	

* This soup can be served hot or cold.

Ingredients
900 g (2 lb) carrots, grated
50 mL (1/4 cup) butter
1 onion, chopped
4 cloves garlic, crushed
1.75 L (7 cups) chicken stock
125 mL (1/2 cup) 35% cream
10 mL (2 teaspoons) sugar
salt and pepper to taste
parsley, chopped

Method
— Melt the butter in a dish at 100% for 1 minute.
— Add the carrots, onion and garlic and mix well; cover and cook at 100% for 4 to 5 minutes, stirring once during the cooking time.
— Stir the mixture and add the chicken stock.
— Cover again and cook at 100% for 1 hour, stirring once during the cooking time.
— Pour into a blender and blend at high speed for several seconds, until creamy.
— Add the cream and sugar and season to taste.
— Refrigerate until ready to serve.
— Sprinkle with parsley before serving.

Note: This soup can be thinned with more chicken stock if necessary.

No magic potions or diabolical ingredients are needed to make this delicious cream soup. Assemble the required ingredients before concocting the soup.

Add the carrots, onion and garlic to the melted butter; cover and cook at 100% for 4 to 5 minutes.

After the first stage of cooking blend in the beef bouillon and continue cooking, covered, at 100% for 1 hour.

Emincé of Veal with Cream Sauce

Level of Difficulty	
Preparation Time	15 min
Cost per Serving	$ $
Number of Servings	8
Nutritional Value	488 calories 28.2 g protein 28.7 g lipids
Food Exchanges	3 oz meat 1 vegetable exchange 1 bread exchange 3-1/2 fat exchanges
Cooking Time	17 min
Standing Time	None
Power Level	100%, 70%
Write Your Cooking Time Here	

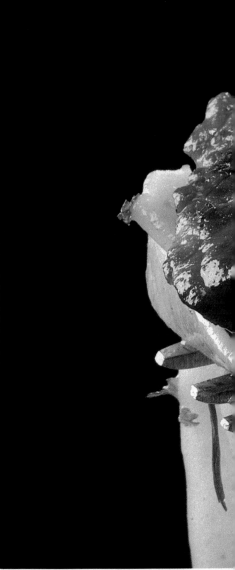

Ingredients

8 veal scallopini, 115 g (4 oz) each
375 mL (1-1/2 cups) 35% cream
60 mL (4 tablespoons) butter
225 g (8 oz) fresh mushrooms, thinly sliced
30 mL (2 tablespoons) lemon juice
125 mL (1/2 cup) chicken bouillon
50 mL (1/4 cup) dry white wine
5 mL (1 teaspoon) paprika
salt and pepper to taste
1 onion, finely chopped
1 L (4 cups) egg noodles, cooked

Method

— Preheat a browning dish at 100% for 7 minutes and add 30 mL (2 tablespoons) butter.
— Sear 4 veal scallopini and set aside.
— Heat the baking dish at 100% for 4 minutes and add the remaining butter.
— Sear the remaining scallopini and set aside with the first four; sprinkle with lemon juice and add the mushrooms.
— Pour the bouillon into the baking dish and heat at 100% for 3 minutes, stirring every minute.
— Add the wine, cream and paprika; stir to mix well.

— Heat at 70% for 5 to 6 minutes, stirring twice during the cooking time (do not let the mixture reach the boiling point).
— Season to taste, cover and set aside.
— Put the scallopini and onion in a dish, cover and cook at 70% for 6 to 8 minutes, moving them halfway through the cooking time.
— Serve the scallopini with the egg noodles and the sauce.

Sear 4 scallopini at a time in a preheated browning dish.

After removing the scallopini, pour the chicken bouillon into the dish. Heat at 100% for 3 minutes, stirring every minute.

Add the wine, cream and paprika; stir and heat at 70% for 5 to 6 minutes.

Jujube Cake

Ingredients
500 mL (2 cups) assorted
jujubes, sliced (exclude black
jujubes)
250 mL (1 cup) golden raisins
125 mL (1/2 cup) butter,
softened
250 mL (1 cup) sugar
2 eggs, beaten
500 mL (2 cups) flour
10 mL (2 teaspoons) baking
powder
1 mL (1/4 teaspoon) salt
175 mL (3/4 cup) milk
5 mL (1 teaspoon) vanilla

Method
— Lightly flour the jujubes
  and raisins; set aside.
— Beat the butter until
  creamy; add the sugar
  and eggs and beat
  continuously, until light.
— Sift the remaining flour,
  baking powder and salt;
  add the dry ingredients to
  the butter mixture,
  alternately with the milk.
— Add the vanilla, raisins

and jujubes; mix well.
— Grease the inside of a 3 L
  (12 cup) tube pan and
  pour in the batter.
— Cover with plastic wrap
  and place the pan on a
  raised rack in the oven;
  cook at 50% for 6
  minutes.
— Remove the plastic wrap
  and cook at 50% for 5 to
  7 minutes.
— Let cool before serving.

Pumpkin Pie

Ingredients
2 20 cm (8 in) pie crusts,
uncooked
1.5 L (6 cups) pumpkin,
cubed
50 mL (1/4 cup) water
250 mL (1 cup) brown sugar
125 mL (1/2 cup) 35% cream
1 small egg, beaten

Method
— Put 1 pie crust in a
microwave-safe pie dish.
— Place the dish on a raised
rack in the oven and
cook at 70% for 5 to 6
minutes, giving the dish a
half-turn halfway through
the cooking time; remove
the dish from the oven
and set aside.
— Put the pumpkin cubes in
a dish and add the water;
cover and cook at 100%
for 10 to 15 minutes, or
until they are cooked.
— Mash the pumpkin cubes.
— Strain the pumpkin
through a sieve, applying
enough pressure to
extract as much water as
possible without forcing
the pulp through.

— Add the brown sugar,
cream and egg to the
pumpkin pulp; mix well.
— Cook at 100% for 4 to 5
minutes, stirring twice
during the cooking time.
— Pour the filling into the
pie crust.
— Cut strips of pie dough
from the other pie crust
and arrange them, criss-
cross, on a piece of
waxed paper.
— Cut around the edges of
the strips of dough, so
that the lattice top is the
same size as the pie.
— Cook at 90% for 1-1/2 to
2 minutes.
— Put the strips of dough
over the top of the pie
and let cool before
serving.

Birthday Favorites

"Just three more days", says little Johnny watching the calendar where he has marked his birthday with a big red X. He knows that on that day, all his friends will come to his house to celebrate with him, that he will be the star of the day and that everyone will be nice to him.

Young and old alike adore birthdays. They are an excuse for happy get-togethers with friends and family. There is no fixed menu for the day: the only rule is to please the tastes of the person who is one year older. So choose a dish which he or she likes, one which will also give the chef a chance to join the party.

While civic or religious holidays are celebrated by everyone together, a birthday is unique for the person celebrating. And so it's normal to try to make this very special day a perfect one, either by showing little Mary how grown up she is or by helping Grampa forget those twelve months which have gone by so quickly.

The menu may vary according to the circumstances and the person, but there are two ironcast traditions. The first is that the meal finish with a dessert, usually an enormous cake, decorated with a candle for every year that has gone by and that all the candles must be blown out at once to make the wish come true. The only exception allowed is to reduce the number of candles on the cake for that lovely older person who still looks so young. Oh yes, the second tradition: don't forget to bring a small gift and to sing Happy Birthday!

From the Recipe to Your Table

Unfortunately, no meal prepares itself. Planning a meal for a number of friends or relatives is hard work and takes organization. Cooking a complete meal in the microwave oven must be planned ahead in the same way as a meal cooked in a conventional oven. Only the cooking and reheating times vary.

The morning of the meal:
—Prepare the coffee mousse.
1 hour 15 minutes before the meal:
—Cook the lamb shoulder. Prepare the orange coleslaw and shrimps in a basket.
10 minutes before the meal:
—Cook the zucchini.

Orange Coleslaw

Level of Difficulty	
Preparation Time	30 min
Cost per Serving	$
Number of Servings	8
Nutritional Value	125 calories 4.4 g carbohydrate 6 g lipids
Food Exchanges	2 vegetable exchanges 1/2 fruit exchange 1 fat exchange
Cooking Time	None
Standing Time	None
Power Level	None
Write Your Cooking Time Here	

Ingredients
1 small green cabbage, grated
4 carrots, grated
30 mL (2 tablespoons) fresh parsley, chopped
250 mL (1 cup) 15% cream
125 mL (1/2 cup) orange juice
pepper to taste
1 clove garlic, finely chopped
125 mL (1/2 cup) raisins
8 black olives
8 segments mandarin orange

Method
— In a bowl, combine the cabbage, carrots and parsley; toss and set aside.
— Combine the cream, orange juice, pepper and garlic to make the sauce.
— Pour the sauce over the vegetables; add the raisins.
— Mix well and divide into 8 equal portions.
— Garnish each serving with an olive and mandarin segment before serving.

This original salad will make all your guests happy. These are the ingredients you will need.

In a bowl combine the cabbage, carrots and parsley.

Combine the cream, orange juice, pepper and garlic to make the sauce.

Pour the sauce over the vegetables; add the raisins.

Shrimp in Baskets

Level of Difficulty	🍴
Preparation Time	15 min*
Cost per Serving	$ $
Number of Servings	10
Nutritional Value	186 calories 7.6 g protein 15.1 g lipids
Food Exchanges	1 oz meat 1 vegetable exchange 2 fat exchanges
Cooking Time	None
Standing Time	None
Power Level	None
Write Your Cooking Time Here	✏️🍎

* Chill before serving.

Ingredients
284 g (10 oz) cooked shrimp
30 mL (2 tablespoons) lemon juice
15 mL (1 tablespoon) dried parsley
salt and pepper to taste
175 mL (3/4 cup) mayonnaise
45 mL (3 tablespoons) chili sauce
30 mL (2 tablespoons) brandy
10 artichoke bottoms
5 stuffed green olives, cut in half

Method
— In a bowl combine the shrimp, lemon juice and parsley; sprinkle with salt and pepper and set aside.
— Combine the mayonnaise, chili sauce and brandy to make a sauce; set aside.
— Fill the artichoke bottoms with the shrimp mixture and pour the sauce over the shrimp.
— Decorate with an olive half before serving.

Combine these ingredients to prepare an exquisite entrée in 15 minutes.

In a bowl, combine the shrimps, lemon juice and parsley. Sprinkle with salt and pepper and set aside.

Combine the mayonnaise, chili sauce and brandy to make the sauce.

Fill the artichoke bottoms with the shrimp mixture and pour the sauce over the shrimp.

Glazed Lamb Shoulder

Level of Difficulty	
Preparation Time	10 min
Cost per Serving	$ $ $
Number of Servings	10
Nutritional Value	326 calories 35.7 g protein 2.3 mg iron
Food Exchanges	4 oz meat 1 fruit exchange
Cooking Time	33 min/kg (15 min/lb) + 1 min
Standing Time	10 min
Power Level	100%, 70%
Write Your Cooking Time Here	

Ingredients
1 lamb shoulder 1.8 kg (4 lb)
125 mL (1/2 cup) 3 fruit
marmalade
5 mL (1 teaspoon) salt
2 mL (1/2 teaspoon) pepper
30 mL (2 tablespoons) flour
30 mL (2 tablespoons)
parsley

Method
— Put the lamb on a tray,
  fat side down and place
  in a dish.
— Combine the marmalade,
  salt and pepper; set aside.
— Cook the lamb,
  uncovered, at 70% for 33
  min/kg (15 min/lb) for
  medium doneness; turn
  the lamb over, dust with
  the flour and brush with
  the prepared glaze;
  continue to cook, basting
  periodically with the glaze
  halfway through the
  cooking time.

⇒

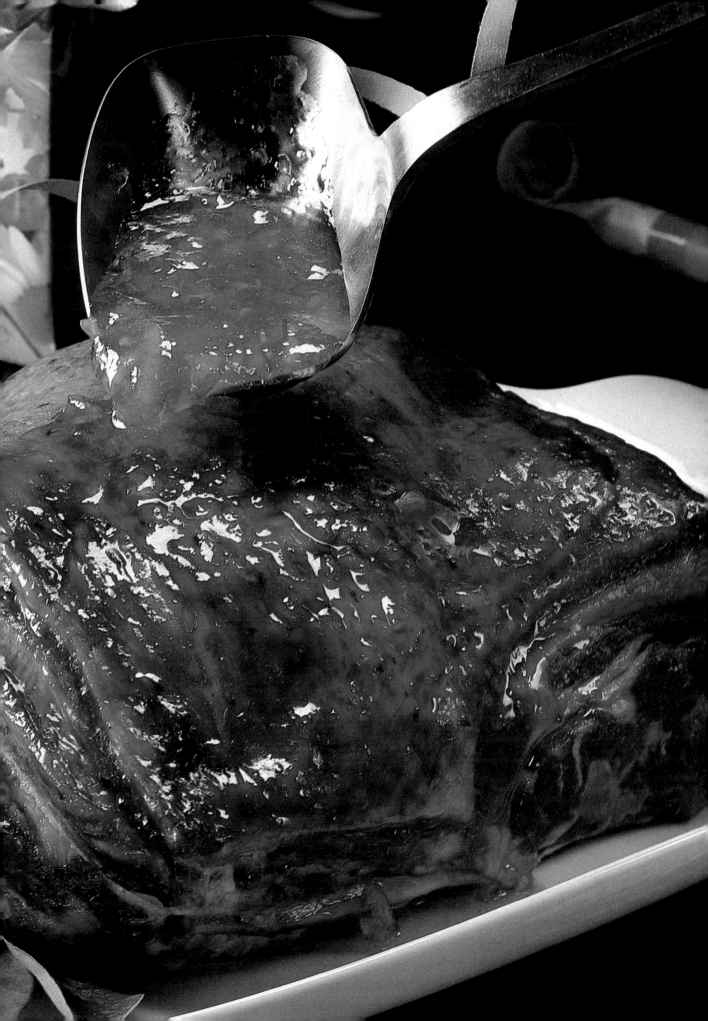

Glazed Lamb Shoulder

— Take the lamb out of the oven; transfer to a serving platter and let stand for 10 minutes.
— Stir the glaze that has dripped into the dish during cooking.
— Heat at 100% for 45 to 60 seconds.
— Pour the glaze over the lamb and sprinkle with the parsley before serving.

MICROTIPS

Using Frozen Vegetables

Frozen vegetables are becoming a more and more important part of our diet because they are so useful. If we don't have any fresh vegetables at home or if we feel like having an out-of-season vegetable in the winter, we can always count on having frozen ones. They keep their beautiful color and their clear taste because they have been blanched in boiling water before being frozen at very low temperatures and they can be cooked in the microwave in no time.

The table on this page indicates the cooking times for some of the most common frozen vegetables.

How To Defrost Half a Package of Vegetables

It's easy to defrost half a package of vegetables in the microwave oven, without affecting the other half of the package. To do this, wrap half the package in aluminum foil and put the whole package in the oven on the defrosting cycle. Then remove the defrosted half, unwrap the aluminum foil, close the package and replace it in the freezer for use at a later time. Finish defrosting the vegetables in a dish.

Cooking Frozen Vegetables at 100% Power

Vegetables	Quantity	Cooking Time (in minutes)
Asparagus	225 g (8 oz)	3 to 4
Beans	225 g (8 oz)	3 to 4
Broccoli	225 g (8 oz)	2 to 4
Brussel sprouts	225 g (8 oz)	3 to 5
Carrots, sliced	225 g (8 oz)	4 to 6
Cauliflower, in pieces	225 g (8 oz)	3 to 5
Corn, kernels	225 g (8 oz)	3 to 4
Corn, ear	1	2 to 3
	2	4 to 5
Spinach	225 g (8 oz)	2 to 3
Zucchini, cubed	225 g (8 oz)	3 to 4

Zucchini with Garlic

Ingredients
4 medium-sized zucchini
125 mL (1/2 cup) garlic
butter
15 mL (1 tablespoon) paprika

Method
— Cut the zucchini in half,
  lengthwise.
— Arrange the zucchini in a
  fan shape on a serving
platter for a decorative
effect or cut into long
strips.
— Heat the garlic butter at
  100% for 1 minute until
  melted; add the paprika
  and stir well.
— Brush the zucchini with
  the mixture.
— Cover and cook at 100%
  for 4 to 6 minutes, giving
  the platter a half-turn
  halfway through the
  cooking time.
— Let stand for 3 minutes
  before serving.

Level of Difficulty	🍴
Preparation Time	10 min
Cost per Serving	**$**
Number of Servings	8
Nutritional Value	117 calories 11.5 g protein
Food Exchanges	1 vegetable exchange 2 fat exchanges
Cooking Time	7 min
Standing Time	3 min
Power Level	100%
Write Your Cooking Time Here	

Coffee Mousse

Level of Difficulty	🍴
Preparation Time	15 min*
Cost per Serving	$
Number of Servings	8
Nutritional Value	124 calories 12.7 g carbohydrate 104.5 mg calcium
Food Exchanges	1/2 fruit exchange 3/4 milk exchange
Cooking Time	8 min
Standing Time	None
Power Level	100%
Write Your Cooking Time Here	

* Chill before serving.

Ingredients
10 mL (2 teaspoons) instant coffee
50 mL (1/4 cup) brown sugar
30 mL (2 tablespoons) cornstarch
15 mL (1 tablespoon) flour
625 mL (2-1/2 cups) milk
3 egg yolks
30 mL (2 tablespoons) butter
1 egg white

Method
— In a bowl, combine the instant coffee, brown sugar, cornstarch and flour; mix well and gradually stir in the milk.
— Beat well and cook at 100% for 6 to 7 minutes, stirring twice during the cooking time.
— Beat the egg yolks; add 50 mL (1/4 cup) of the coffee mixture.
— Stir in the rest of the hot mixture and heat at 100% for 1 minute.
— Whisk in the butter.
— Cover the mixture with a sheet of plastic wrap, laid directly on the surface.
— Let cool.
— Whip the egg white to stiff peaks; fold into the cream mixture.
— Pour the mousse into cups and place in the refrigerator to chill.

MICROTIPS

Making a Great Mousse

Sometimes even the most carefully prepared mousse will stubbornly refuse to set, without one quite knowing why. The reason for this may be that some fresh fruits, such as pineapple, contain enzymes which counteract the effect of the gelatin. In this case, the fruits should first be cooked (cooking destroys the enzymes) or replaced with jams.

For a more full-bodied mousse, you can add some liqueurs. Madeira, for example, adds character to apricots and coffee liqueur will bring out the full flavor of mocha. Sweet white wine, kirsch, maraschino and even champagne can also be used.

Adding Volume to Egg Whites

Egg whites kept in the refrigerator have less volume than egg whites kept at room temperature. To remedy this situation, put egg whites that have been kept in the refrigerator into the microwave oven at 100% for 10 seconds. Do not cook any longer as they will toughen.

Christmas Treasures

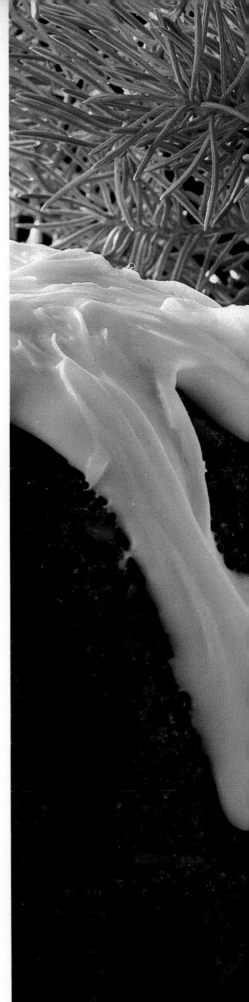

Candles burning slowly in the middle of a beautifully set table with a red cloth; background music of carols and traditional hymns; a proud pine in the corner of the room, decked out in all its finery and bright lights, surrounded by colorful wrapped presents; frosted windows through which snowflakes can be seen, softly falling . . .

In a moment the scene will come to life. The guests will arrive. The central element of these get-togethers with family or friends, or even of a romantic tête-à-tête, is a well-dressed table. For no other holiday, except perhaps New Year's Day in some countries, is the food as important. On this occasion, everybody pulls out their old recipe books and prepares unending shopping lists. And on the special day, all diets are temporarily abandoned. Precious wines are brought up from the cellar and cooks try their very best to surpass one another. After all, the evening of December 25 occurs only once a year. Over time, every country has acquired special Christmas recipes.

Everywhere, cakes and pastries hold the place of honor and culinary tradition has endowed us with a great many recipes for these special confections. In this volume, we offer a recipe for individual mocha cakes for your menu. Also on page 101 and on the following pages you will find suggestions for adding variety to your Christmas menu: a potato and parsnip gratin, a shrimp pâté, glazed vegetables and gingerbread men.

From the Recipe to Your Table

Unfortunately, no meal prepares itself. Planning a meal for a number of friends or relatives is hard work and takes organization. Cooking a complete meal in the microwave oven must be planned ahead in the same way as a meal cooked in a conventional oven. Only the cooking and reheating times vary.

The night before the meal:
—Prepare the sole mousse, Christmas salad, tourtière and mocha cakes.
The morning of the meal:
—Prepare the shrimp pâté.
3 hours before the meal:
—Cook the stew.
40 minutes before the meal:
—Cook the potato and parsnip gratin.
20 minutes before the meal:
—Cook the glazed vegetables.
5 minutes before the meal:
—Reheat the tourtière.

Sole Mousse

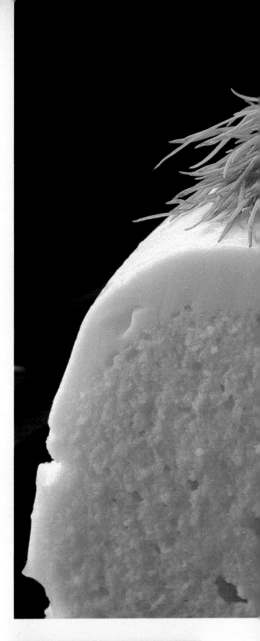

Level of Difficulty	🍴🍽
Preparation Time	15 min
Cost per Serving	$
Number of Servings	8
Nutritional Value	260 calories 15.7 g protein 21.5 g lipids
Food Exchanges	2 oz meat 2-1/2 fat exchanges
Cooking Time	25 min
Standing Time	5 min
Power Level	50%
Write Your Cooking Time Here	✏️🍎

Ingredients
450 g (1 lb) filet of sole, cut in pieces
250 mL (1 cup) 15% cream
5 eggs
4 egg whites
30 mL (2 tablespoons) butter, softened
250 mL (1 cup) 35% cream
salt and pepper to taste

Method
— Combine the fish, 15% cream and all the eggs and egg whites in a blender; purée until smooth.
— Add the butter and the 35% cream; blend again and season to taste.
— Grease the inside of a tube pan and spoon in the mixture.
— Place the pan on a raised rack and cook at 50% for 22 to 25 minutes, giving the dish a half-turn twice during the cooking time.
— Let stand for 5 minutes; serve with a Hollandaise sauce.

To prepare this delicate dish which all your guests will surely enjoy, first assemble these ingredients.

Use the blender for a smooth, creamy mixture.

Place the pan on a raised rack and cook at 50% for 22 to 25 minutes.

Give the dish a half-turn twice during the cooking time.

Christmas Salad

Level of Difficulty	
Preparation Time	30 min*
Cost per Serving	$ $
Number of Servings	10
Nutritional Value	195 calories 2.2 g protein 36.6 g glucids
Food Exchanges	1 oz meat 2 fruit exchanges
Cooking Time	9 min
Standing Time	None
Power Level	100%
Write Your Cooking Time Here	

* The salad is cooled during preparation and then refrigerated before serving.

Ingredients
22 mL (1-1/2 tablespoons) unflavored gelatin
50 mL (1/4 cup) cold water
250 mL (1 cup) hot water
375 mL (1-1/2 cups) sugar
1 L (4 cups) cranberries
15 mL (1 tablespoon) lemon juice
175 mL (3/4 cup) chopped nuts
250 mL (1 cup) celery

Method
— Sprinkle the gelatin over the cold water; set aside.
— Pour the hot water into a casserole and add the sugar; heat at 100% for 3 minutes to dissolve the sugar.
— Add the cranberries and cook at 100% for 4 to 6 minutes, or until the cranberries burst.
— Add the lemon juice and gelatin; stir carefully.
— Let cool.
— When the mixture is just about set, add the nuts and celery.
— Rinse a mold in cold water and pour in the mixture.
— Refrigerate until set.

This original recipe will certainly bring you many compliments. These are the ingredients you will need.

Sprinkle the gelatin over the cold water; set aside.

Add the lemon juice and gelatin to the cranberries; stir carefully and let cool.

Pigs' Trotters Stew

Ingredients
8 pigs' trotters
hot water
1 onion, grated
1 bay leaf
5 mL (1 teaspoon) pork
spices
salt and pepper to taste
175 mL (3/4 cup) toasted
flour
250 mL (1 cup) cold water

Meatballs:
1 onion, grated
125 mL (1/2 cup) bread,
crusts removed, crumbled
1 egg
675 g (1-1/2 lb) lean ground
pork
salt and pepper to taste
1 mL (1/4 teaspoon) fine
herbs

Method
— Split the rind of the pigs'
  trotters and put them in a
  casserole.
— Cover with hot water;
  add the onion, bay leaf,
  pork spices, salt and
  pepper.
— Cover and cook at 100%
  for 40 minutes.
— Stir the pigs' trotters and
  cover the dish again; set
  the power level to 70%

and continue cooking for
40 to 60 minutes, or until
the meat comes away
easily from the bone.
— Remove the pigs' trotters
  and put them aside;
  discard the bay leaf.
— Combine the toasted
  flour and cold water and
  add to the cooking juices.
— Cook uncovered at 100%
  for 15 to 20 minutes until
  thickened, stirring every 5
  minutes; set aside.
— To prepare the meatballs,
  put the onion in a dish,
  cover and cook at 100%
  for 1 to 2 minutes,
  stirring once during the
  cooking time.
— Soak the bread in the
  egg.
— Add the ground pork;
  season with salt and
  pepper, then add the fine
  herbs and grated onion.
— Form into meatballs.
— Return the pigs' trotters
  to the casserole and add
  the meatballs.
— Cook at 100% for 10 to
  15 minutes, or until the
  meatballs are cooked,
  stirring twice during
  cooking time.

Tourtière

Ingredients
1 pie crust
1 egg yolk
5 small triangles cut from
cooked pie dough

Filling:
450 g (1 lb) lean ground pork
125 mL (1/2 cup) water
1 mL (1/4 teaspoon) sage
1 mL (1/4 teaspoon) dry
mustard
1 mL (1/4 teaspoon) cloves,
ground
1 onion, finely chopped
1 clove garlic, crushed
salt and pepper to taste

Method
— In a 2 L (8 cup) casserole,
combine all the
ingredients for the filling
and mix well.
— Cook uncovered at 100%
for 8 to 10 minutes, or
until the mixture is
cooked, stirring every 3
minutes during the
cooking time.
— Let cool for 20 to 30
minutes.
— Drain off the excess
liquid.

— Put the pie crust in a
microwave-safe pie plate.
— Brush the inside of the
crust with the egg yolk.
— Pour the filling into the
crust and garnish the
surface with the triangles
of dough.
— Cook uncovered at 70%
for 4 to 5 minutes, or
until the tourtière is hot,
giving the dish a half-turn
halfway through the
cooking time.

Potato and Parsnip Gratin

Ingredients
900 g (2 lb) potatoes, peeled
and thinly sliced
450 g (1 lb) parsnips, peeled
and thinly sliced
225 g (8 oz) carrots, sliced
75 mL (1/3 cup) water
2 onions, finely chopped
175 mL (3/4 cup) milk
175 mL (3/4 cup) 18% cream
1 egg, beaten
1 mL (1/4 teaspoon) mace
salt and pepper to taste
30 mL (2 tablespoons) butter
125 mL (1/2 cup)
breadcrumbs

Method
— Put the potatoes,
parsnips and carrots in a
dish; add the water and
cover.
— Cook at 100% for 8 to 10
minutes, stirring once
after 5 minutes.
— Drain the vegetables
carefully and arrange
them in rows in a
casserole; sprinkle with
the onion and set aside.
— In a bowl, combine the
milk, cream, beaten egg
and mace; season to taste

with salt and pepper and
pour over the vegetables.
— Put the butter in a small
bowl and heat at 100%
for 30 seconds until
melted; add the
breadcrumbs and mix.
— Sprinkle the breadcrumb
mixture over the
vegetables.
— Cook at 100% for 4 to 6
minutes, giving the dish a
half-turn halfway through
the cooking time.
— Let stand for 3 minutes.

Shrimp Pâté

Ingredients

115 g (4 oz) can shrimps,
drained
50 mL (1/4 cup) butter
3 cloves garlic
15 mL (1 tablespoon) white
wine
115 g (4 oz) cream cheese
2 green onions, finely
chopped
50 mL (1/4 cup) fresh
parsley, chopped
pepper to taste

Method

— Put the butter in a small
dish; heat at 100% for 1
minute or until melted.
— Place all the other
ingredients in the
container of a blender.
— Pour in the melted
butter. Purée until
smooth.
— Refrigerate and serve with
crackers or bread.

Glazed Vegetables

Ingredients
250 mL (1 cup) carrots,
thinly sliced
250 mL (1 cup) rutabaga,
thinly sliced
60 mL (4 tablespoons) butter
10 broccoli flowerets
10 cauliflower flowerets
50 mL (1/4 cup) orange juice
1 mL (1/4 teaspoon) nutmeg
salt and pepper to taste

Method
— Put the carrots, rutabaga
and butter in a casserole;
cover and cook at 100%
for 5 to 6 minutes,
stirring once during the
cooking time.
— Add the broccoli,
cauliflower, orange juice
and nutmeg.
— Cover and continue
cooking at 100% for 3
minutes.
— Uncover, stir and cook at
100% for 3 to 4 minutes,
stirring twice during the
cooking time.
— Season to taste and let
stand, covered, for 2
minutes.

Mocha Cake

Ingredients
125 mL (1/2 cup) butter
250 mL (1 cup) sugar
3 egg yolks, beaten
3 egg whites, beaten to stiff
peaks
500 mL (2 cups) flour
10 mL (2 teaspoons) baking
powder
125 mL (1/2 cup) milk
5 mL (1 teaspoon) vanilla

Mocha Frosting:
250 mL (1 cup) butter
2 egg yolks
1 to 1.25 L (4 to 5 cups) icing
sugar
125 mL (1/2 cup) strong
coffee
375 mL (1-1/2 cups)
almonds, thinly sliced

Method
— Cream the butter; add the
  sugar and beaten egg
  yolks; fold in the beaten
  egg whites.
— Combine the flour and
  baking powder and add
  to the butter mixture,
  alternating with the milk,
  mixed with vanilla.
— Grease a 20 cm (8 in)
  square pan and spoon in
  the batter; cover the
  corners with aluminum
  foil.
— Put the pan on a raised
  rack and cook at 70% for

4 minutes.
— Remove the aluminum
  foil and give the pan a
  half-turn; cook at 70%
  for 3 to 4 minutes.
— Let cool and cut into 16
  squares.
— To prepare the frosting,
  cream the butter and add
  the egg yolks.
— Add the sugar, alternately
  with the coffee; beat until
  creamy.
— Use to frost the tops and
  sides of the small cakes;
  sprinkle with almonds.

Gingerbread Men

Ingredients
125 mL (1/2 cup) shortening
150 mL (2/3 cup) fancy
molasses
500 to 625 mL (2 to 2-1/2
cups) flour
10 mL (2 teaspoons) ground
ginger
5 mL (1 teaspoon) cinnamon
2 mL (1/2 teaspoon) baking
soda
2 mL (1/2 teaspoon) salt

Method
— Cream the shortening.
— Gradually add the
  molasses.
— Sift the remaining
  ingredients and beat into
  the shortening to form a
  stiff dough.
— Refrigerate for 1 hour
  then roll the dough out
  with a rolling pin.
— Cut into 10 pieces in the

shape of a man.
— Arrange 5 pieces on a
  plate and place on a
  raised rack in the oven.
— Cook at 70% for 2 to
  2-1/2 minutes, giving the
  dish a half-turn halfway
  through the cooking time.
— Repeat the procedure
  with an other 5 pieces.
— Decorate to taste before
  serving.

The History of Entertaining

On the Tables of Rome

The Romans are famous for their love of good living. Of course, when they were fighting their first wars, their meals were more frugal. It was only later, when their empire extended to Africa, Sicily and Greece, that they began to exploit local riches. From then on they adopted new habits. The Romans brought back new dishes they had discovered in far away lands and the citizens of Rome developed a taste for these new foods and new methods of preparation.

Roman feasts were impressive not only for the variety and quantity of food served, but also for their luxurious surroundings. Atmosphere played an important role: the room where the feast was held was fragrant with a thousand exotic scents, the number of courses became incalculable, the waiters (slaves at that time) were innumerable.

With the opening of the trade routes, oriental herbs and spices were imported to Europe by sailors and merchants alike and these spices are still used in our dishes. Onion, cumin, coriander, pepper, sage, chervil, chives, cinnamon, mint, oregano, thyme, dill, marjoram, cardamom and fennel, to name just a few, are the same spices mentioned in the most ancient cookbook known. Attributed to the Roman, Apicius, this book was probably written between the first and third centuries B.C.

Court Food and Cottage Food

In the Western world, wine has long been served at feasts and has always been a part of any entertaining. Alcohol, on the other hand, is a fairly recent product. Its use only began to spread in the 17th century. It was also at that time that several other products of modern life, which would call vices, began to appear, including coffee, tobacco and sugar.

When Catherine of Medici married Henry II, Italian cooking entered the kingdom of France, for she arrived in 1533 accompanied by her Florentine cooks. In one swift move, modern cooking gained its patent of nobility. A century later, during the reign of Louis XIV, banquets followed one another in dizzy succession. Restless and extravagant chefs competed in imagination and daring to offer edible works of art to the Court. Brillat-Savarin, in his book, *The Physiology of Taste,* published in 1825, describes feasts of the time at which thousands of fish and birds were served and the courses included ''a dish made of the brains of five hundred ostriches and another prepared with the tongues of five thousand birds''.

Indeed, gastronomy was the product of the Court. But the ''cooking of the people'', too, has always had a place in history for it has remained faithful to tradition throughout the centuries, while gastronomy was subject to the whims of fashion and changed with the seasons.

Royal Menus, from the Fourteenth Century to Elizabeth II

People have always been fascinated by the meals of royalty. The abundance, quality and rarity of the foods served, as well as the originality of the preparation, are all part of the mystery surrounding the king's table. Like more modest cooking, royal cooking was in constant evolution, as you can see from the three authentic menus presented here.

In the fourteenth century, for example, a menu which was the wonder of the German people seems quite accessible to us.

On the other hand, at the beginning of the fifteenth century, in the time of Charles VI of France, gastronomy was marked by extravagant food and abundant courses. Nowadays, royal banquets such as those at Buckingham Palace are still special events. But it's easy to see that they are influenced by new trends and changes in our attitude towards food. The dishes are lighter and healthier. This new approach, which royalty shares with the common folk, tends to pay more attention to a food's natural flavors and nutritional values.

Fourteenth Century Menu, Served in Honour of Bishop Zeiz, in Germany

First Course
Egg soup with saffron, pepper and honey
Millet soup
Mutton with onions
Roast chicken with prunes

Second Course
Cod with oil and raisins
Fried plaice
Boiled eel with pepper

Third Course
Boiled or roasted fish
Small larded birds fried with radish
Ham with cucumbers

Menu of a Meal Served to King Charles IV

First Course
Capons with cinnamon
Chicken with herbs
New cabbage
Venison

Second Course
Roast joint
Peacock
Capon pâté
Hare with rose vinegar
Capons in must

Third Course
Partridge with clover
Braised pigeons
Venison pâté
Jellies and tarts

Fourth Course
Creams
Pear pâté
Almonds
Sweet tarts

Two Menus Prepared at Buckingham Palace for Queen Elizabeth II

Menu 1
Cream of sorrel
Sole Veronica
Beef fillet Medici
Peas with butter
Potato croquettes
Salad Lorette
Cold soufflé Empereur
Chocolates
Fruit

Menu 2
Charentais melon
American salmon
Roast lamb with rosemary
Fresh peas
Green beans
New potatoes
Salad
Mocha bombe

Entertaining Terminology

Chocolate pot: A container for melted chocolate.

Cruet set: Two containers in a stand, one for oil and one for vinegar to serve at the table.

Faience: A type of earthenware made from an opaque paste which is then painted or enamelled.

Fish slice: Sharp spatula used to cut and serve fish.

Fruit nappy: Cup-shaped dish, used to serve jams or fruits.

Ladle: Large spoon with a long handle and a deep round spoon used to serve soups.

Lazy susan: A revolving tray for serving condiments or food.

Place setting: The grouping of plates and cultery used by each guest.

Porcelain: Translucent, impermeable substance used to make fine china.

Ramekin: Small dish for oven or double-boiler cooking, also used for serving.

Sauce boat: Small dish used for serving sauces and gravies.

Tureen: A broad, deep dish with a cover, used for serving soups and stews.

Conversion Chart

**Conversion Chart for the
Main Measures Used in
Cooking**

Volume
1 teaspoon . . . . 5 mL
1 tablespoon . . . . 15 mL

1 quart (4 cups) . . . . . . 1 litre
1 pint (2 cups) . . . . . . 500 mL
1/2 cup . . . . 125 mL
1/4 cup . . . . 50 mL

Weight
2.2 lb . . . . 1 kg (1000 g)
1.1 lb . . . . 500 g
0.5 lb . . . . 225 g
0.25 lb . . . . 115 g

1 oz . . . . 30 g

**Metric Equivalents
for Cooking
Temperatures**

49°C . . . . 120°F	120°C . . . . 250°F
54°C . . . . 130°F	135°C . . . . 275°F
60°C . . . . 140°F	150°C . . . . 300°F
66°C . . . . 150°F	160°C . . . . 325°F
71°C . . . . 160°F	180°C . . . . 350°F
77°C . . . . 170°F	190°C . . . . 375°F
82°C . . . . 180°F	200°C . . . . 400°F
93°C . . . . 200°F	220°C . . . . 425°F
107°C . . . . 225°F	230°C . . . . 450°F

Readers will note that, in the recipes, we give 250 mL as the
equivalent for 1 cup and 450 g as the equivalent for 1 lb and
that fractions of these measurements are even less
mathematically accurate. The reason for this is that
mathematically accurate conversions are just not practical in
cooking. Your kitchen scales are simply not accurate enough
to weigh 454 g—the true equivalent of 1 lb—and it would be
a waste of time to try. The conversions given in this series,
therefore, necessarily represent approximate equivalents, but
they will still give excellent results in the kitchen. No problems
should be encountered if you adhere to either metric or
imperial measurements throughout a recipe.

Index